REAL AND TRUE

Hope for the Restless Heart

REAL AND TRUE
Hope for the Restless Heart

Dear Alice,

Blessing and Hope,

Chloe and Linda Grabeman

Chloe & Linda Grabeman

REDEMPTION
PRESS

Published by Redemption Press, PO Box 427, Enumclaw, WA 98022

Toll Free (844) 2REDEEM (273-3336)

Redemption Press is honored to present this title in partnership with the author. The views expressed or implied in this work are those of the author. Redemption Press provides our imprint seal representing design excellence, creative content, and high quality production.

All Scripture quotations, unless otherwise indicated, are taken from The Message. Copyright © 1993, 1994, 1995, 1996, 2000, 2001, 2002. Used by permission of NavPress Publishing Group.

ISBN 13: 978-1-68314-115-0 (Print)
978-1-68314-116-7 (ePub)
978-1-68314-117-4 (Mobi)

Library of Congress Catalog Card Number: 2017937199

Dedicated to every longing heart and restless soul searching for truth, satisfaction, and purpose in this life.

HERE'S THE DEAL

We've both been told we have peaceful, gentle spirits and we hope this book reflects those qualities. You don't have to read these chapters in order. Rather, read them as you need to. If you are feeling weary, then read the chapter on renewal; if fearful, read the chapter on courage. Wherever you need a heaping dose of hope, you'll find it here.

DON'T EVEN THINK ABOUT SKIPPING THIS CHAPTER!

You Won't Understand the Book

Welcome to hope. Have you been seeking it? Longing for it? Afraid you'd never find it? Well you have. If you could use some rest, some hope, some truth, you're in the right place. The door on the front cover says, *You're Welcome Here.* So come in. Put your feet up. Grab a beverage. Relax.

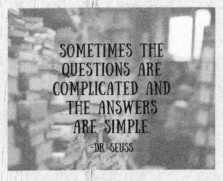

SOMETIMES THE QUESTIONS ARE COMPLICATED AND THE ANSWERS ARE SIMPLE.

-DR. SEUSS

We all get restless for hope, for meaning, for peace. We get caught up in things that drag us down or tie us up. Things that call us away from who we are. But not only do we run to things not worthy of our time, we stay too long at things that are good... and end up worn out and spent. Ever been there? That's when we know it's time to rest. If that's where you are, come unplug with us for a while.

Would you like an adventure now or shall we have our tea first?
-Peter Pan

Join our conversation, because no one likes being left out. We'll even give you a name in this conversation. *Restless Heart.* Because we're sure you are like us. Once in your life you've probably asked yourself, *Is this all life is? Am I doing it right? Can I ever stop those voices in my head?* You may be anywhere from twenty to eighty years of age, but whatever your age or heart situation, we welcome you into a friendship with two other hearts who have felt that same longing.

Tell the negative committee that meets inside your head to

SIT DOWN AND SHUT UP!

Oh, and we have names too. We are Expectant Heart, a twenty-something, and Experienced Heart, a Baby Boomer. To break the ice, here are some silly little things about ourselves. Kind of like eating spaghetti or corn on the cob on a first date, we want you to know exactly who we are—without any false illusions—right off the bat. Meet us and our quirks. We think you'll like us. Isn't that where friendships often begin? We'll do age before beauty. So here goes:

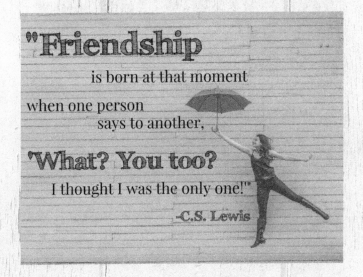

"**Friendship** is born at that moment when one person says to another, 'What? You too? I thought I was the only one!'"

-C.S. Lewis

Experienced Heart:

- *Thrilled that 60 is the new 40.*
- *Bleached blonde and appropriately wired for that stereotype.*
- *Slightly to seriously disorganized. Wrote notes for this book on the vomit bag of a plane.*

- *Madly in love with my husband; passionate about my three children.*
- *Way too fond of pink and pretty things.*
- *Convinced that God shows up, even in hard times.*
- *Pinching myself that I get to write a book with my daughter.*

Expectant Heart:
- Lover of all things coffee, Gilmore Girls, the color green, and Ben Rector related.
- I find quite a lot of joy in finding new music and telling people about it.
- If you have; a) a quick wit, b) mastered the art of sass, or c) make me laugh, we will be quite good friends.
- The jumpiest person you will ever meet.
- Currently a student at Lee University living in the library.
- I'm still awestruck that God truly delights in me.
- Equally as giddy to be writing a book with my momma!

There is one more voice in this book, but that voice has no age. He is Eternal Heart, and here are a few wonderful facts about Him:

Eternal Heart:

- MORE IN LOVE WITH YOU THAN YOU COULD EVER WISH OR IMAGINE.
- ALONGSIDE YOU WHETHER YOU FEEL HIM OR NOT.
- AWARE OF YOUR WORST FAULTS AND BIGGEST MESS-UPS . . . AND LOVES YOU STILL.
- WAITING TO TALK WITH YOU ANY TIME AND ANYWHERE.
- THE TRUE AUTHOR OF THIS BOOK.

This isn't a normal book. Instead of pages upon pages of endless text, it is chock full of pictures and graphics, songs and tweets. And we unabashedly admit that portions of this book are not original, but they are used in a new and fresh way. In *Steal Like an Artist*, Austin Kleon said, "Nothing is completely original." How true that is, because he is simply restating what Solomon said centuries ago when he penned, "There is nothing new under the sun" in Ecclesiastes 1:9. So, enjoy our collage of what we've tweaked and made our mark on; adaptations of things we've loved combined with thoughts straight from our hearts. Not every word, picture, or tune will fit your life. That's ok. Take in what you like and leave the rest.

One last thing...

Why Music?

As you read this book you will find that music has been added for your discovery. Here's the reason. You may or may not notice all our chapter titles are John Mayer songs. I have had a lifelong love for John's music. My guitarist brother Carey idolized the man, so I can honestly say I grew up with John. We are buds. In our younger days, if you ever overheard a conversation between Carey and me, we were probably talking about John's incredible song writing and guitar skills. It was a family obsession. Growing up with Carey, constantly surrounded by his music or other artists, his love for music slowly became mine too.

In my opinion, music is one of the most powerful forces in this world. In the words of my dear friend Sophie, "Even people who don't have anyone in their life feel accompanied by music. It's like the therapist that doesn't have a consultation but is there for you 24/7." Lyrics can give language to the moments of life that leave you speechless. They can help you heal, give you joy, and bring back the light of hope in your life. Music has been one of my main sources of communication in my walk with God.

The songs I have provided in each chapter have all taught me something and helped me get through the hardest of seasons. I have listened to them countless times,

I can't explain but I'll find a song that can

letting the lyrics wash over me, quenching my thirsty soul. This is our desire with the different forms of media that bind our book together. We want you to connect in every way possible to the many ways God communicates with us.

Love,
Expectant Heart

P.S. Look up complete *Real and True* playlist on Spotify!

One

NEW DEEP

What is this *Hope Thing?*

Dear Restless Heart,

Get ready. If living life on your own terms hasn't worked, then you are in the perfect place to read this book. If you are sick of big promises and self-help formulas, keep turning these pages. If you've tried to fill your life with this world's hope and found it fictitious, disappointing, and exhausting, then it's time to experience the real thing.

All my life my heart has yearned for something I cannot name

We'll address questions that matter at the end of the day...with humor, honesty, and different perspectives. Maybe you've tried living by the world's rules. You've taken your best shot at its beliefs and so-called benefits and found them empty. Maybe the accepted cost of success is just too high for you—the striving too intense, the satisfaction too momentary. Then you're on the right track.

Because it's not all about you and it's not all dependent on you. Here's the shocker: Whatever you have dreamed of, whatever you have run after, you've also been pursued. But not only pursued. Desired. Longed for, in fact. To give you hope. Real hope. True hope. Calm in place of turmoil. Certainty instead of questions. Unchanging truths in place of temporary fads. You're going to be surprised at what you find in this book. But it's all good.

Love,
Experienced Heart

HOPE POINT #1 – There is more to this life than you ever imagined—more joy, more meaning, more hope, and it's all offered to you.

Hope

Dear Restless Heart,

Do you ever get sick of yourself? Ever feel like you're always a disappointment? Do you catch yourself striving to "get your life together" but constantly falling through the cracks? Then it's time to lay your efforts down. Welcome to *Real and True*. We want to tell you about a hope that can't be found in the fleeting things of this world, because well, we've been there. We've been restless. We've felt the fear when faced with the future. <u>We know</u> <u>the shame and</u> <u>failure in com-</u> <u>parisons.</u> <u>Strug-</u> <u>gles</u> with <u>love,</u> <u>courage,</u> and <u>forgiveness</u> have been familiar scenarios on our yellow brick road. And <u>we know</u> <u>the quest for</u> <u>renewal can be</u> <u>everything but</u> restful.

"You would have not called to me unless I had been calling you," said the Lion.

-C.S. Lewis, The Silver Chair

Hope

No matter what your lifestyle, whether you're a Baby Boomer ex-perienced heart like Momma, or a twenty-some-thing expectant heart like me, restlessness is all too familiar. Our desire is that you come to know the

Hope is the thing with feathers that perches in the soul and sings tunes without the words and never stops at all

-Emily Dickinson

heart of our steadfast, loving hope and his heart for you. It's time to close the window of the old whispers saying you're a disappointment, and open the door to the hope that calls you by a name you have all but forgotten. So please come in and rest for a while.

Love,
Expectant Heart

#madehopeful

Song List -

1. *Crave* - For King and Country
2. *I Have this Hope* - Tenth Avenue North
3. *Now More Than Ever* - Brandon Heath
4. *Fierce* - Jesus Culture
5. *The Lion and the Lamb* - Big Daddy Weave
6. *Washed by the Water* - NEEDTOBREATHE

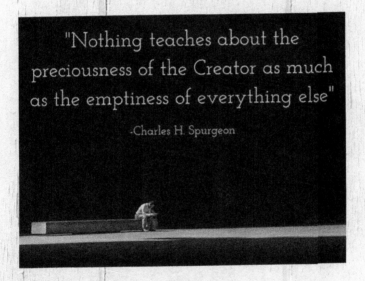

"Nothing teaches about the preciousness of the Creator as much as the emptiness of everything else"

-Charles H. Spurgeon

23

DEAR RESTLESS HEART,
*SO DON'T YOU SEE THAT WE DON'T
OWE THIS OLD DO-IT-YOURSELF LIFE
ONE RED CENT. THERE'S NOTHING IN
IT FOR US, NOTHING AT ALL. THE BEST*

*THING TO DO IS GIVE IT A DECENT
BURIAL AND GET ON WITH YOUR NEW
LIFE. GOD'S SPIRIT BECKONS.*

ROMANS 8:12-14

LOVE,
ETERNAL HEART

Two

WHY GEORGIA

Thirsty for Perfection

Dear Restless Heart,

We all want perfect lives. Spouses or significant others who totally understand us; children who surpass all others; careers or callings which excel and fulfill. And we want all of that on our time-table and our own terms. But even worse, we are surprised and disappointed when we don't get it just that way.

Pain is real. But so is hope.

That's the bad news. Here's the good news: God knows all our longings. He un-derstands what we want and why we want it. He has seen our searching, our striving, our fretting. The countless ways we pretend, to others and to ourselves that we're fine...just fine. And He cares, even when we say, "I've got this, God. Don't need Your help, but thanks anyway." We so often end the conversation with the Eternal Heart. Door shut. God left outside.

What we don't understand is that ending that communication opens one of a distinctly different nature. A conversation with one who seems so enticing at first, so full of promises. They are never quite as they seem, though. Here's one of his favorite lies:

Everybody has a chapter they don't want to read out loud.

Favorite Lie

"Let me tell you the truth about this God. Yeah, He may love you, but He's disappointed in you. How many times are you going to make that same mistake? Can't you get your life together? By this age, you should be over that. God's had it with you."

26

And we fall for it! We feel terrible, so we spend endless energy trying to prove our value. That we are good. And worthy. Important. It becomes a driving force in our lives, even though we'd never admit it. It's exhausting.

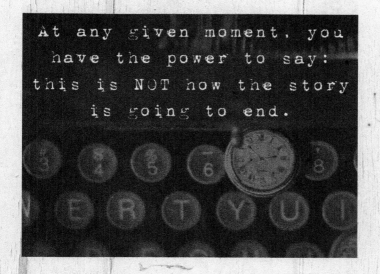

At any given moment, you
have the power to say:
this is NOT how the story
is going to end.

27

Our response to this big, fat lie that tries to make us believe in a God who is never satisfied, always grumpy, and out to get us. Who would want a God like that? Not us. Only truth can dispel a lie, so here it is: (Yes) we've all chosen selfish paths and been preoccupied with ourselves...our desires, our goals, our fulfillment. We have closed the door and allowed the dialogue with the Divine to stop. But here's His real response: He is not angry or even disappointed. He's heartbroken. He misses talking to us. And He is patiently, passionately waiting to start that conversation again.

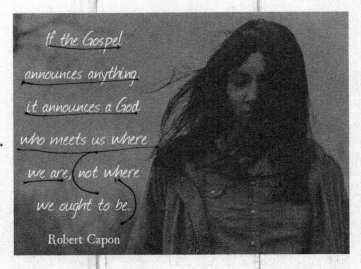

If the Gospel announces anything, it announces a God who meets us where we are, not where we ought to be.

Robert Capon

Yea!

28

Are you willing to open that door and let Him into your life? His Father-heart is relentlessly kind and surpassingly gracious. Aren't you ready for chats like that? For an end to the condemnation? In its place, love like you've never experienced. Then I'll tell you the words He spoke so clearly to me in prayer as I began writing this book: Tell them that I love them! Tell them that I love them.

Tell them I love them.

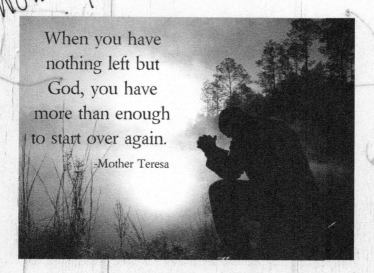

When you have
nothing left but
God, you have
more than enough
to start over again.
-Mother Teresa

Now don't think I'm some lunatic. I didn't hear an actual voice, but in my heart, I heard Him loud and clear. And if you get nothing else from this book, get this: God loves you. On your good days and on your worst ones. Regardless, *He loves you. He moved heaven and earth to prove it to you.* That, dear friends, is the true heart of the Father. For you. But there's so much more. Keep reading.

Love,
Experienced Heart

You've got a new
story to write

and it looks nothing
like your past

Hope Point #2 – Regardless of where you are or what you've done, God's relentlessly kind heart loves you without measure, without change, and without end.

Dear Restless Heart,

Do you ever look at your friends and just wish you could have a better hold on your life like they seem to have? Do you feel like you lack something and are running so far behind the crowd that you will never catch up and surely never succeed in life? Are you burdened with intimidation and performance? Then this reading is for you from someone who knows this battle all too well.

TWO THINGS PREVENT US FROM HAPPINESS:

Living in the past

AND OBSERVING OTHERS

We are surrounded with mirrors that pop up at the most inopportune moments to tell us everything we lack. They can have many names but at the root of all of them are the mirrors of <u>Looks</u> and <u>Works</u>. They mock us and chain us, plugging our ears from the truth God says about us. My mirrors started to pop up at me in college. I could be surrounded by the wonderful group of guys I've been blessed with as close friends, and out of nowhere a mirror would pop up with its judgmental whispers, *You know you're not good enough to have a guy like this pursue you, right?*

31

Or I could be among a group of people and after a while feel the introvert in me become exhausted and anxious to leave. Then Mr. Mirror would catch up to me, *Chloe, you keep leaving after an hour! Come on! Why aren't you more of an extrovert like them?*

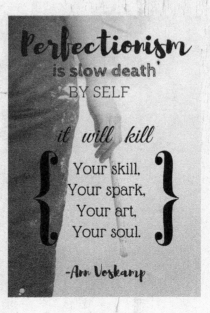

Perfectionism
is slow death'
BY SELF

it will kill

{ Your skill,
Your spark,
Your art,
Your soul. }

-Ann Voskamp

Our actions usual-
ly revert to one
thing, thanks to
these controlling
mirrors - perfor-
mance. We begin
to strive so hard

Performance

Her success is not my failure

to be the best Christian, friend, parent, employee,
or spouse. God's will quickly turns steep, narrow, and
rocky for us, and we find ourselves on a tightrope
where one wrong move messes up everything, re-
sulting in God's disappointment. Ever felt that way?

32

How can emptiness be so heavy?

These are the dangers of comparison. Our life
becomes an exhausting race to perfection. I spent
much of my life living this way without even realizing

it. If someone would ask me what my biggest fear was I would say screwing up God's plans for me. But it is not supposed to be like this! God wants you to smash your mirrors of Looks and Works because they are tools from the enemy. They make you work and perform for God's approval when you already have it! Mirrors give you misconceptions about God, making Him look distant and demanding, putting too much power in your hands when it has always belonged in His.

> You can spend your whole life trying to be deserving of what God has already made you worthy of
>
> —Steven Furtick

I came home from my sophomore year of college with these feelings weighing down on my shoulders. A dear friend and pastor at my church, Thad

Barnum, asked me to talk to him about my year and how I had gotten to this low point. After I told him all these fears and feelings he asked me, "Chloe, does that look like the loving, kind, and patient God you serve?" He offered me a different image of God's will.

A funny thing happened when I finally let go God intervened.

That God is more like a ballroom dancer wanting to teach us the steps to the beautiful dance He has choreographed for us. He knows we will not get every step perfectly and He is patient to help us along the way. No matter how many times we may step on His feet. He leads from behind with His hand on our back, keeping each of us steady in His

34

arms. When we dance with our Father, keeping our eyes on Him instead of any of the other dancers, we find our freedom and delight in Him. He knows us perfectly and requires no perfection from us. He offers His

35

presence, love, acceptance, and guidance as freely as a dancer extends his hand. I don't know about you but I am tired of performing and feeling like I am never enough. It is time to smash the mirrors this world throws at us and find our true worth in the freedom God has given us!

Love,
Expectant Heart

#mademe

Song List:

1. *Through and Through* - Will Reagan
2. *Priceless* - For King & Country
3. *Hesitate* - Judah and the Lion
4. *Running into Freedom* - Will Reagan
5. *All He Says I Am (feat. Kari Jobe)* - Cody Carnes
6. *This Love* - Housefires

DEAR RESTLESS HEART,
[THEY] MET GOD OUT LOOKING FOR
THEM! GOD TOLD THEM, "I'VE NEVER
QUIT LOVING YOU AND NEVER WILL."
EXPECT LOVE, LOVE, AND MORE LOVE!

JEREMIAH 31:3

LOVE,
ETERNAL HEART

Three

ON THE WAY HOME
Thirsty for Change

Dear Restless Heart,

It has been rightly said that at the heart of life is a timeless love story: God created a world and a family, lost that family, and then paid an inexplicable price to win it back. He's always known we couldn't do this life alone. He never planned for it to be lived without Him. But we walked away. So, He let us try it solo. But in many ways, the world has misled us.

Drove my Chevy to the levee but the levee was DRY
Don McLean

You may be confused about this whole God-thing, and honestly, you are afraid to begin talking with Him again. He can handle your confusion. Just be real with Him. If you are ready to give up this self-reliance and allow God to be more than a brokenhearted bystander to your life, He will welcome you wholeheartedly back into hope.

IT WOULD BE SO NICE IF SOMETHING MADE SENSE FOR A CHANGE.

—LEWIS CARROLL
ALICE IN WONDERLAND

38

All you must do is welcome Him into your thirsty places. Years ago, I had a real-life analogy about thirst. I don't remember hearing about the value of drinking a lot of water when I was growing up, so when I tried it as an adult, I didn't feel thirsty. The truth, though, was that I was totally dehydrated; I just didn't realize it. Only when I purposely chose to drink more water did I even develop my sense of needing it. Maybe that's where you are with God. You have no idea just how badly you need Him. All of who He is: loving, giving, forgiving, renewing.

Have that initial (or often repeated) conversation with Him about those places which never seem to feel satisfied, where you wonder what the meaning of it all is anyway. Areas of your life you try not to think about too much. Just start with the first one that comes to your mind, and tell God. Tell Him about those empty, dry places where you long to be quenched. Where you are always thirsty. You must be dry somewhere or you wouldn't have picked up this book. Tell Him. He'll meet you right there. We promise. His heart breaks for our brokenness and He knows how to heal it.

We all drink lies when our hearts are thirsty...

40

You are about to meet eight individuals who were thirsty in various ways. They just lived their lives. They had not one inkling that their struggles would become stories of hope. None. But they did, and they do and they will...until stories are told no more. These God-was-here-after-all glimpses were recorded for us. For our hard times. For our are-you-kidding-me moments when we ask, "Where are you, God? Do you even care what's going on here?" These eight conversations give us a resounding answer from Heaven, "I do care. And I am here. And you're not alone." God showed up. Every time. Amid real life. Real, messy, full-of-drama life.

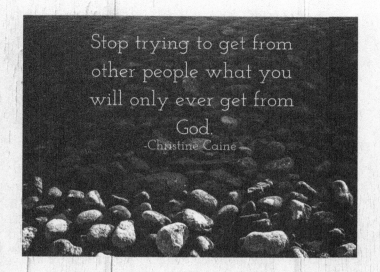

Stop trying to get from other people what you will only ever get from God.
-Christine Caine

You'll find yourself in these next chapters. Find yourself in the heartbreak of confusion or fatigue, strained relationships or guilty-as-sin hearts. And you'll meet the solution. The solution with a name. Jesus. He's the new character about to enter our conversations. Actually, He's the main character. And the hero. He gets us talking to God again. Gives us the chance to get back on track — with God, with others, with ourselves. He always initiates the conversation. For these eight people, for us. Because of Him there's no more working to make God happy. No more apologies or excuses. Just receiving and believing. And then following.

Love,
Experienced Heart

Hope Point #3 – God has done the unimaginable by sending Jesus to renew the conversation that was ended, reclaim us as His own, and restore our broken lives.

Dear Restless Heart,
Like you, we understand life can be full of thirsts pulling us this way and that to wells of love, success, and wholeness. But these worldly wells we are drawing from give water which seeps through the cracks of our leaky buckets leaving us with restless hearts and thirsty souls. Well restless heart, we are writing to you because we've filled our buckets full but come up empty too. Our goal is to offer you hope and satisfaction in the one true fount.

LIKE THE WOMAN AT
THE WELL,

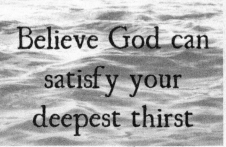

Believe God can
satisfy your
deepest thirst

So, what does a restless, thirsty heart look like? It can look like a heart longing for love and identity. A puppet bound by strings of perfection and comparison. A worn soul with a lost life-purpose. A prisoner chained to the past and its burdens, longing to break free.

> If I find in myself desires which nothing in this world can satisfy, the only logical explanation is that I was not made for this world.
>
> -C.S. Lewis

God gives us a picture of someone who embodied this restlessness. The woman at the well. She filled her buckets with everything this world had to offer. Love, relationships, you name it, she drank it. But that afternoon at the well, Jesus looked past her shoddy reputation and saw only her restless heart. He said to her, "Give me a drink." Maybe this drink is really an invitation to Himself. Maybe He is saying, "Give me a drink. Give Me a try. Drink on Me. You've drank from so many wells and they have all run dry. Drink on Me and never

43

go thirsty again!" Her restless heart replies, "Sir, you have nothing to draw water with, and the well is deep." What I believe she really means is, "Sir you do not want me giving you water. You don't want to get into my mess of a well, my mess of a life... it's too deep with dirty water and mistakes. I could never be good enough to drink from your well."

"...and to wake up knowing God is on my side is enough."

44

But the thing is, you can never be good enough to drink from Christ. That's a given. But like the woman at the well, Jesus sees straight to your restless heart and invites you to Himself. Come, muddy water and all, and find rest from your restlessness.

Leave your leaky buckets at the door and find true satisfaction in the one true fount. Trust me, you won't be able to contain your satisfaction!

Love,
Expectant Heart

#madesatisfied

Song list:
1. *Love is Here* – LIVE – Tenth Avenue North Live: Inside and In Between
2. *Never Run Dry* – Housefires
3. *All I Ever Needed* – AJ Michacka
4. *You are More* – LIVE – Tenth Avenue North Live: Inside and In Between
5. *Mars* – Joseph Holm
6. *Come to the River* – Housefires
7. *Lost is Found* – Joseph Holm

DEAR RESTLESS HEART,
I'LL MAKE A COVENANT OF PEACE WITH THEM THAT WILL HOLD EVERY-THING TOGETHER. I'LL LIVE RIGHT

THERE WITH THEM. I'LL BE THEIR GOD! THEY'LL BE MY PEOPLE!

EZEKIEL 37:26-27

LOVE,
ETERNAL HEART

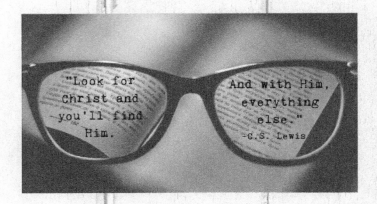

Four

WAR OF MY LIFE
Thirsty for Salvation

Dear Restless Heart,

Have you ever had a long weekend that absolutely blew your mind? As if time slowed down and sped up all in the same moment, leaving you breathless. Breathless and different. Not the same person on Sunday as you were on Thursday. Changed so much that life would never be the same again? If you've ever felt that way, you're not alone. It's happened before. To real people.

Eight lives were careening down a cliff. Life as they had imagined it had come screeching to an abrupt halt. But Jesus met them in their topsy-turvy reality and He restored their equilibrium. He can do the same with us. He still restores hope when life takes a serious plot twist.

WHEN SOMETHING GOES WRONG IN YOUR LIFE, JUST YELL, "PLOT TWIST!" AND MOVE ON.

48

The first of these eight characters was a thief. He shared a hill bearing three crosses with a man named Jesus. The thief may have been close to his last breath. Before, he had yelled insults at Jesus, along with the thief on His other side. But now, he understands much more. He recognizes that he is a supporting character in the pivotal moment of all history. His sin, along with that of the rest of humanity have been picked up, willingly, by this Jesus, the Nazarene. This man suffering on the cross next to him must surely be the

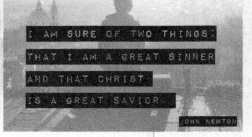

I AM SURE OF TWO THINGS: THAT I AM A GREAT SINNER AND THAT CHRIST IS A GREAT SAVIOR.

JOHN NEWTON

Messiah. Before, the thief showed Him only rudeness and reviling; now he makes a request: "Jesus, remember me when you come into your kingdom."

And all it took was that one appeal. Jesus' immediate response was, "Don't worry, I will. Today you will join me in paradise." Instantaneous acceptance; immediate welcome. And suddenly, this unnamed thief has a name: Redeemed. Saved. Forgiven. Actually, all of the above. I'll bet for just an instant his excruciating pain was relieved because the ache in his heart was finally healed. This man who had done everything wrong in his life — run hard and fast from the law and the Lord, now declared not guilty by the Judge of all the earth. All it took was opening up and asking Him in.

49

The meaning of life. The wasted years. The poor choices of life. God answers the mess of life with one word: grace.

This unnamed robber teaches us three vital lessons. First, it's never too late until one's final breath. Next, we can never be too bad for Jesus. By his own admission, this man knew his guilt. It was heavy enough to deserve crucifixion. Jesus was unfazed. He gave forgiveness and salvation instantly. Third, it's never too hard a task. It is the same formula for the thief as for us: Realize your need, acknowledge His power, and ask for His help. All it takes is a conversation. But it's a crucial one. If you've never had that talk, do it today.

> Grace was free, but that doesn't mean it was cheap. You were bought with a cost; that cost was the cross.

Years ago, I had a body builder speak at my children's school. He fascinated the children with his brute strength as he bent a steel rod around a *little girl's waist. He captivated us with his story of Jesus' strength over his debilitating addiction and sadness. His t-shirt read, Eternity is too long to get wrong. He was right. Don't get it wrong. Have that conversation with Jesus. Today. Give Him your heart. Just like the thief, you'll be glad you did for a very, very long time. Eternity, in fact.*

Love,
Experienced Heart

51

Satan will say,
"You have all the time in the world to
get right with God"...he lies.

Hope Point #4 – Jesus did what we could never do – live a perfect life, bringing us a perfect salvation, all because of His amazing grace.

Dear Restless Heart,
Ok, we're about to get real. I mean *really* real. Get ready because this chapter is about burdens. We all have them. Those dark. disgusting places deep in our bones that cause us regret and shame. They lock us in chains as they replay memories of our past, weighing us down, making us slaves to their terrifying whispers. They trap us in constant fear. What would happen if the world knew the truth? The truth of all we have done, all we have said, all the places we have wandered off and the slow fade that has led us to where we are today. There is no place that feels more alone.

The Devil knows your name but calls you by your

SIN

God knows your sin but calls you by your

Name

-Ricardo Sanchez

Before I fully embraced my faith at age fifteen, there were some choices I felt shame and regret over. Living in all that fear, shame, and regret, hearing the truth of the gospel didn't seem possible for me. I would hear things like, "Christ died for you so He could take away all your sins," or "Jesus can take all of you, all your shame, all your past, and make you new! No sin is too big for God." But I felt like I was too far gone. This is a scary place, with no hope. But one day I reached the end of myself. I was so weary of feeling dirty and exhausted from my sins. I finally stopped fighting and surrendered, and for the first time in a long time I felt free.

The thing is, when talking about freedom from burdens, we become even more scared because we know we are going to have to confess all these dark places. But we hold back because we think those chains that keep us from truly living must be better than what God or anyone else would say when they find out the truth.

If you haven't noticed from the song lists thus far, I am a huge fan of Tenth Avenue North. I was listening to one of their YouTube playlists, and Mike, the vocalist, was sharing a conversation he had had with his wife about some burdens she was scared to tell him. It was so difficult for her to tell him, but when she finally did, Mike's immediate response was, "That's it?" We get so trapped in our fear of what God and others will think if they know the truth, we can't even imagine that someone would reply "That's it" to our story. We believe we are the worst of the worst and His grace could never cover our sins. The phrase that keeps us away from God, in our chains, can be summed up in five words: "You don't know my story." I have said those words myself but I have finally realized what a lie from the pit of hell they are.

54

How beautiful it is that God still pursues us when we are running from Him

One thing I find so beautiful about the Bible is its timelessness. So many of its characters were also bound by the phrase, *You don't know my story.* But these people are proof that God loves broken people. *Loves* them. *Wants* them. And *uses* them for His glory. Their stories categorize them as the worst of the worst as well, but God always gets down on their level and uses them for mighty things. To give you a few examples, Rahab was a prostitute; David, Moses, and Paul were all murderers; Matthew cheated people; Jacob was probably a pathological liar; Sampson had a weakness for women; Solomon struggled with sexual immorality (majorly); and Peter betrayed Jesus.

He died because He thought you were priceless...and you think you are worthless?

The point is, God tends to use people who have done the worst things for His greatest glory because more than anyone they have experienced the power of God's grace over sin. Paul puts it perfectly in I Timothy 1:15, "Here's a word you can take to heart and depend on: Jesus Christ came into the world to save sinners. I'm proof – Public Sinner Number One – of someone who could never have made it apart from sheer mercy." Jesus is a loving savior. You need to know that Christ had you on His mind when He was crucified. With every whip to His side or nail in His limbs, He knew He was one step closer to you becoming His. He drank in your sin and embodied your darkness and shame so He could wash you clean and pronounce you blameless. He already knows your story, and trust me, He is big enough to handle it. There is a way for Christ to free you, love you, and forgive you and He has willingly, lovingly paid that price.

Love,
Expectant Heart

#madeclean

Song List -

1. *New Beginnings* - Luminate
2. *Mended* - Matthew West
3. *Won't Give Up* - Colony House
4. *I'm not who I Was* - Brandon Heath
5. *Beautiful Things* - Gungor
6. *You Love me Anyway* - Sidewalk Prophets
7. *O Come to the Altar* - Elevation Worship
8. *Fighting for You* - Tenth Avenue North
9. *Oh my Dear* - Tenth Avenue North
10. *At the Table* - Josh Garrels

57

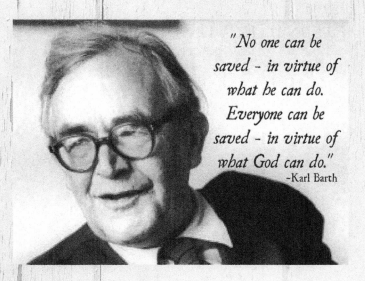

"No one can be saved - in virtue of what he can do. Everyone can be saved - in virtue of what God can do."
-Karl Barth

DEAR RESTLESS HEART,
COULD IT BE ANY CLEARER? OUR
OLD WAY OF LIFE WAS NAILED TO
THE CROSS WITH CHRIST, A DECI-
SIVE END TO THAT SIN-MISERABLE
LIFE - NO LONGER AT SIN'S BECK AND
CALL! WHEN JESUS DIED, HE TOOK
SIN DOWN WITH HIM, BUT ALIVE HE
BRINGS GOD DOWN TO US.

ROMANS 6:6, 10

LOVE,
ETERNAL HEART

Five

IN REPAIR
Thirsty for Belief

Dear Restless Heart,
He couldn't even go there in his mind. Not in his wildest dreams. Oh, he wanted to. With every fiber of his just-leave-me-alone soul, he wanted to. But if he let himself believe... and it was wrong... he'd have to begin grieving all over again. So, he barricaded his heart as much as he had barricaded himself.

Nothing, not one thing had turned out the way Thomas thought it would. In the past three days, just one short weekend, everything he had called certain, normal, and life-giving had been snatched from his life. His friend and rabbi, Jesus, was gone. Judas Iscariot had sold him out to the religious elite for the price of a slave. Jesus and the disciples had shared bread and wine and then He had washed their feet. They went to a familiar place to pray. Judas had left early. Betrayal was his agenda. And here he came with the Pharisees, the Roman soldiers, weapons and torches to apprehend Jesus in the garden at Gethsemane as if He were a criminal. Then, oh, what a nightmare it was! The illegal trials, the trumped-up charges, the floggings. And the next day, He was crucified. Too much to comprehend. Too much grief, too much shock, too much pain.

60

The very last people Thomas wanted to see were the other ten disciples. They reminded him of all the stories, the laughter, the Good Friend. He just wanted to be alone. He did what we so often do when life doesn't follow our expected agenda. He

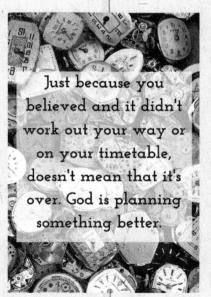

Just because you believed and it didn't work out your way or on your timetable, doesn't mean that it's over. God is planning something better.

checked out. Stopped talking to the other disciples. Isolated himself. He needed out-of-sight-out-of-mind to work just this one time. He didn't expect the next event though. They told him they'd seen Jesus. Alive! That He had shown up in the room where they were meeting...possibly that same room where He had washed their feet on Thursday. But just hearing wasn't good enough for him. He needed to see the scars on Jesus' hands and feet for himself. He couldn't bear to be disappointed again.

Only God knows what drew him back to his friends. But somehow, God got him back there. To that room. Because that was the only way for healing to begin. For restoration to take its first step. You have to go back to the painful places and let Jesus meet you there.

And He did. Jesus showed up eight days later! All the disciples were together again, including Thomas. And Jesus had an appointment to keep. With Thomas. To prove Himself to him. To meet him right where he was...heartbroken, disillusioned, confused. To answer all those emotions in the same way... with grace. Jesus gladly gave him exactly what his heart needed to see in order to believe—a glimpse of His hands and side.

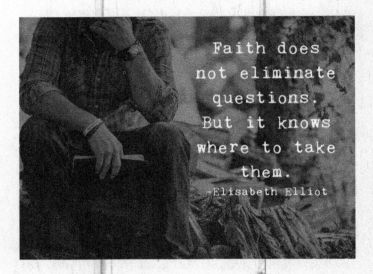

Faith does not eliminate questions. But it knows where to take them.
-Elisabeth Elliot

He will treat each of us with that same gentle grace when we despair. Lose faith. Want to run away. He never expects us to have a one-size-fits-all faith. Even if we're the only ones who don't believe. No. His is a tailored-just-for-you approach. Always. It made all the difference for Thomas. He who had been slow to believe was the very first to proclaim that Jesus was his Lord and God.

"If you don't have doubts
you're either kidding
yourself or asleep. Doubts
are the ants-in-the-pants of
faith. They keep it moving."
-Frederick Buechner

63

Don't let Thomas-thoughts keep you from God-chats. Jesus can handle whatever emotion we are feeling. But we need the honesty of Thomas. No masquerading. No whitewashing. No charades. Soul healing will happen just as tenderly as it did for Thomas. He no longer doubted. He now had unshakeable faith. All because of a conversation with Jesus.

Love,
Experienced Heart

Hope Point #5 – God loves to prove Himself to us when we are honest about our doubts, questions, and disappointments.

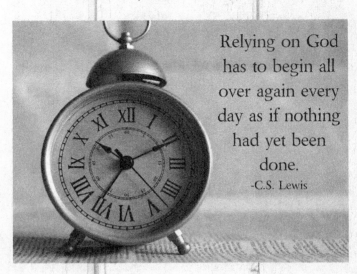

Relying on God has to begin all over again every day as if nothing had yet been done.

-C.S. Lewis

Dear Restless Heart,

Have you ever had a nickname from one unfortunate moment of your life that is now permanently stuck to you? Maybe *spaz, chubs, drama queen?* Or maybe something more drastic, more shameful: *drunk, cheater, liar?* Somehow your whole identity is known by one moment of weakness and heartbreak. This disciple of Jesus is known all too well by a permanent nickname – *doubting Thomas.*

Doubt. The secret struggle of the Christian life, covered in guilt and shame. It is hardly ever voiced because the obvious solution of course is, "You need more faith in God. Just lay it at His feet." "Thanks. Now my eyes are open and problems solved."

Let's get real. Doubt is a lot more complex than this. Thomas understood its power like no other. In John 20:25 the true human nature of doubt is laid bare. The sticky label of *doubter* is attached when he exclaims his need to place his finger in Jesus' scars in order to believe. Thomas actually had such hope in Jesus. He was his teacher and his friend, but he never expected in his wildest dreams that

Jesus would die for him. The only one who had the power to raise the dead had just been horrifically murdered and Thomas was left with the wind knocked out of him, heartbroken.

Heartbreak is the hardest place to have faith. We don't know where to go when it comes flooding in. He couldn't go to his comforter; he was just killed. And he didn't dare go back to the other disciples, his brothers. No matter where he turned, Thomas was reminded of Jesus. So, what did he do? He retreated into himself and tried to find the answers warring within -- alone. Can you relate to Thomas? Has your current circumstance left you with doubt...and shame from what God may think of your doubt? Do you have nowhere to go but into yourself? Then it's time we look at doubt with a new lens. Have you ever really stopped to think of how Jesus met Thomas in his doubt?

Someday you'll be really, really grateful that God gave you what you needed instead of what you wanted.

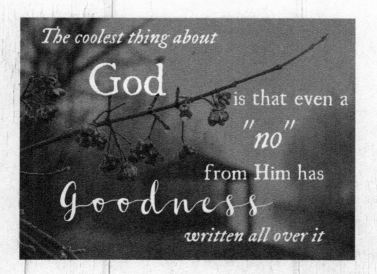

The coolest thing about *God* is that even a "*no*" from Him has *Goodness* written all over it

Jesus came to him and to the other disciples even though the doors were locked. He unlocked doors of isolation without even having a key. Then, without a second thought or judgment, he told Thomas to put his fingers in His scars. Jesus was so willing to show Thomas the holes in His hands and prove Himself to Thomas' doubt. There was no guilt placed on Thomas. No claims of His disappointment, no angry reminders of Jesus' miracles that Thomas had seen. Just kindness and love.

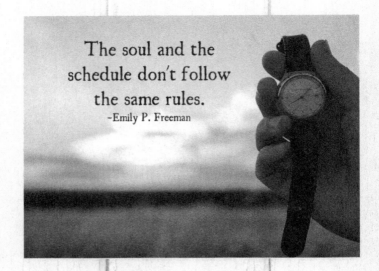

The soul and the schedule don't follow the same rules.
-Emily P. Freeman

Jesus stands with us as well and comforts us, meeting us in our loneliness and heartbreak. Doubt can be a burden and a gift. God turned Thomas' experience of doubt into the most relatable part of his testimony. What would we ever do without Thomas? When we are sifted through the sands of doubt we can, in the end, be convinced of what is most important. I heard a pastor put it this way, "The voice of God and the voice of doubt can and should coexist." When we are sifted through the sands of doubt the God who emerges from the struggle is nothing of our own safe crafting, but rather a God of renewing power and never ending kindness to meet us in our questions. Will you allow

God to meet you in your doubts, heartbreak, and isolation? Will you let Him take your sticky, shameful nicknames and make them something mighty?

Love,
Expectant Heart

#remade

Song List -

1. *Hold My Heart* - Tenth Avenue North
2. *By your Side* - Tenth Ave North
3. *Give me. Faith* - Elevation Worship
4. *Close Behind* - Joseph Holm
5. *In Control* - Hillsong United
6. *Closer* - Lifepoint Worship
7. *When Darkness Falls* - Jenny and Tyler

The voice you believe will determine the future you experience.

-Steven Furtick

DEAR RESTLESS HEART,
THE SPIRIT OF GOD, THE MASTER, IS ON ME BECAUSE GOD ANOINTED ME. HE SENT ME TO PREACH GOOD NEWS TO THE POOR, HEAL THE HEARTBROKEN...TO CARE FOR THE NEEDS OF ALL WHO MOURN...GIVE THEM BOUQUETS OF ROSES INSTEAD OF ASHES, MESSAGES OF JOY INSTEAD OF NEWS OF DOOM.

ISAIAH 61:1-3

LOVE,
ETERNAL HEART

MY STUPID MOUTH
Thirsty for Forgiveness

Dear Restless Heart,

Peter. He is always listed first in the ordering of Jesus' disciples. Every time. He would have certainly put himself at the end of the list on that horrible, promise-breaking night of Jesus' arrest. In fact, in his mind, he didn't even qualify to be on that list. Have you ever had self-examinations where you fail with flying colors? I have. That's the thing about forgiveness; to pick it up, we must lay down the recriminations which we are so prone to wrap snuggly around ourselves. Yes, he had messed up. Been a big mouth, arrogant, swear-up-and-down, perfect-in-his-own-mind follower as Jesus washed his feet and gave him the bread and wine. But the night went on. And it got hard. Too many questions trying to link him to Jesus. Fear overcame his once-faithful heart. He denied Jesus. Not once. Not twice. Three times. Just like Jesus said he would. He was tested and he failed.

> If He chooses not to remember our sins,
>
> **WHY DO WE KEEP SHAMING AND BLAMING OURSELVES FOR THEM?**

72

In my mind, this conversation with Jesus is the dearest, kindest one, because it is done in private. It is mentioned a few times in the Bible, but no details are given. We are only told that it happened. Jesus meant it to be that way. He had every right to run Peter over the coals for what he did. Could have justifiably made him grovel in front of all the other disciples who had heard his boastful promises. But Jesus didn't act like that. He knew the depth of Peter's pain and He dealt with it from the depth of His kindness. He unlocked and released those chains of guilt, disgust, and embarrassment. Now they lay cold on the ground, shackling Peter no more.

You can know the joy of that freedom too. Because here's the truth about Peter's denial: Jesus knew he would do it. He had told him. He wasn't surprised. He wasn't disappointed. He had always known it was coming that night. Just as He knows every sin we will ever commit. They don't catch Him off-guard. Does that shock you?

Remember that favorite fable of Satan's, the one that goes like this: "Yeah, God loves you, but He is really disappointed in you"? That one. He can't be disappointed in us if He already knows how we will act. It doesn't even make sense if you think of the all-knowing nature of God. Every thought, every word, every action. We act precisely as He knows we will. And He loves us still.

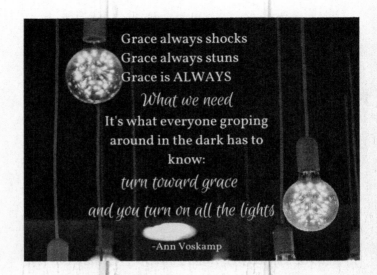

Grace always shocks
Grace always stuns
Grace is ALWAYS
What we need
It's what everyone groping
around in the dark has to
know:
turn toward grace
and you turn on all the lights

-Ann Voskamp

74

All those places where we beat ourselves up either for what we've done or what we haven't done, we need to settle them once and for all with Jesus. We didn't shock Him. He isn't upset with us. He just wants to free us, forgive us, and empower us to move on...just like He did for Peter. All it takes is a one-on-one conversation with Him.

Love,
Experienced Heart

Hope Point #6 – God's love for us is based not on who we are, but on who He is: overwhelmingly gentle, outrageously good, and overflowing with grace.

Sure you can have
a second chance.
Just ask Peter.

MAX LUCADO

Dear Restless Heart,

Can you imagine what it must have been like when Peter heard the rooster crow? Seeing Jesus' face after his final betrayal left his lips? Peter. Jesus' right hand man, the leader of the disciples, the one who would have gone to the ends of the earth for Jesus, had just betrayed Him three times — just as Jesus predicted. Have you ever hit that moment? Been knocked full force by the consequences of your actions? You hate to even look at yourself in the mirror. Disgusted, horrified, filled with shame, like Peter when he saw Jesus, all you can do is run.

How do we deal with the shame? How do we ever approach our perfect and pure God when it feels we are covered with a permanent layer of thick, dirty,

> God will convict you in order to change you, but never accuse you in order to shame you.
> —Steven Furtick

black-as-night sin? How do we live with ourselves? How do we forgive ourselves? Our natural response is to try to clean ourselves up. Even if we have sinned, at least we can show God we are doing damage control. We do every good deed, try to lighten the blackness of our sin so maybe one day we can stand before God again. Exhaustion is now the only thing as loud as the shame.

Forgiving yourself can be much more difficult than forgiving others. But the truth is, like Peter, you were made for more, so much more than your un-forgiveness. Have you ever thought about both betrayals in Jesus' death? Judas sold Jesus to the religious authorities to be killed. Peter denied ever knowing Jesus. Two sins that cut deep and were equally grave in God's eyes. After all the guilt and shame that nearly consumed these two disciples, we see their stories ending quite differently. Judas' story ended with a noose around his neck. Peter's story began his role as the leader of the church, forgiven by Jesus, and forgiven by himself. So, what happened? What made the difference?

Unconditional grace, love, and forgiveness happened. In some ways, these are such foreign concepts to us. They sound too good to be true. But the truth is God is not done with you just because you think you have fallen too far. Jesus rarely responds to our shortcomings the way we think He will. When we think He will respond with disappointment, He meets us with kindness. When we think we will re-ceive rejection, He pulls us close with salvation. For Peter, Jesus could have disowned him, could have mocked him and said, "I told you so!" But instead Jesus continued His walk to death, for Peter and for you. He knew the only thing that could wash away your sin-stained hands was His blood. So, He paid the price for your forgiveness. This was not an angry purchase that covers you in debt to Him but rather, a purchase of love to free you. And

Peter finally accepted it. Judas could never forgive himself and he was met with death. Peter finally let go and believed he was forgiven because Jesus said he was. He was met with life more full than he could have ever imagined.

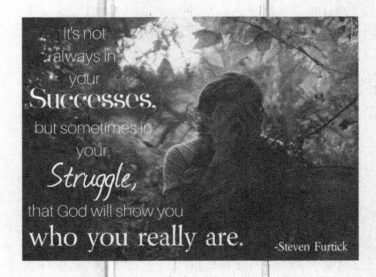

It's not always in your **Successes,** but sometimes in your *Struggle,* that God will show you **who you really are.** -Steven Furtick

So, Restless Heart, it's time you know that you can let go. You can forgive yourself because you are forgiven by the One who sees you in quite a mightier way than you see yourself. You are not the worst sinner that ever was and God is not finished with you. Not even close. No more asking for for-giveness over and over again. No more self-hatred.

No more haunting memories of the past. Just pure freedom.

Love,
Expectant Heart

#madefree

Song List -
1. *Come Away* - Jason Polley
2. *Beautiful the Blood* - Kutless
3. *Clearing Stones* - John Lucas
4. *You Loved me Anyway* - Sidewalk Prophets
5. *Only Grace* - Matthew West
6. *Running into Freedom* - Will Regan
7. *We are Forgiven* - Elevation Worship
8. *Who You Are* - Unspoken
9. *That's how you Forgive* - Shane and Shane

DEAR RESTLESS HEART,
WHERE IS THE GOD WHO CAN COM-
PARE WITH YOU - WIPING THE SLATE
CLEAN OF GUILT. TURNING A BLIND
EYE, A DEAF EAR TO THE PAST SINS OF
YOUR PURGED AND PRECIOUS PEOPLE?

YOU DON'T NURSE YOUR ANGER AND DON'T STAY ANGRY LONG, FOR MERCY IS YOUR SPECIALTY. YOU'LL STAMP OUT OUR WRONGDOING. YOU'LL SINK OUR SINS TO THE BOTTOM OF THE OCEAN.

MICAH 7:18-19

LOVE,
ETERNAL HEART

80

Dear Past,
Thank you for the lessons.
Dear Future,
I'm now ready.

Seven

DREAMING WITH A BROKEN HEART
Thirsty for Love and Identity

Dear Restless Heart,

Broken hearts. Sometimes they are masked behind bad behavior. We respond negatively. Jesus sees right through to the woundedness, the longing, the insatiable need to be accepted. I'm just surmising, but I think I have good evidence. Not once, not twice, not even three times, but five different times John proudly placed this self-stick label on his chest: "The disciple whom Jesus loved." Perhaps John had tried to win his earthy father's approval all his young life. In his early twenties now, he may have feared that Jesus would find him unacceptable too.

I wonder if John had issues with love and identity. He and James were brothers, sons of Zebedee. They lived in Galilee, which was a big fishing village. We deduce from several facts that their father had a prosperous fishing business. What if Daddy was rarely home, or stayed too busy for his little boys?

God approved of you before anybody else ever got a chance to disapprove.

Maybe a difficult relationship with their dad was the reason John and his brother James grew up to be hotheads. Jesus had given them the nickname "Sons of Thunder," and fittingly so. For instance, when the people in one town had not welcomed Jesus, James and John wanted to call down fire from heaven on them. Uh-oh! Jesus had some work to do on these boys.

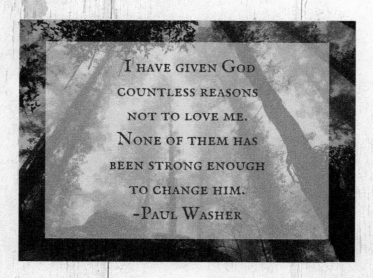

I HAVE GIVEN GOD
COUNTLESS REASONS
NOT TO LOVE ME.
NONE OF THEM HAS
BEEN STRONG ENOUGH
TO CHANGE HIM.
-PAUL WASHER

John soaked up the love of his Savior like a dry, parched sponge for three and a half years. Surely this young, wounded heart received healing from Jesus' unconditional love. He was certainly a different man by the end of his life, having realized beyond his wildest dreams that Jesus really, really loved him. No longer a son of thunder. Now, "the disciple of love." His Gospel and even more, his three letters, I, II and III John, were all about the transforming reality, power, and ministry of God's love. He knew it well. He had experienced it. Now he gladly gave it to others. All because of conversations with the one called the Comforter, the Counselor.

"and this is the
marvel of all
marvels;
that he called
me Beloved."
- C.S. Lewis

Each of us needs that same comfort somewhere in our lives. In some way, we could use that counsel. We may even have a self-stick label that we need to have removed or reworded. All it takes is time with Him.

Love,
Experienced Heart

Hope Point #7 – With God, our identity is always secure and we always know where we stand. We are His and we are loved.

GOD LOVES YOU UNCONDITIONALLY AS YOU ARE AND NOT AS YOU SHOULD BE, BECAUSE NOBODY IS AS THEY SHOULD BE.

-BRENNAN MANNING

85

Dear Restless Heart,
At the core of your being, who do you believe yourself to be? What have you identified yourself with? When all is stripped away, at the heart of your existence, what do you believe to be absolutely true? What do you call yourself? Maybe honest? Or motivator? Maybe failure? Or undeserving? Unloved?

Dealing with who you believe yourself to be is a different deal than who others have come to call you, through sticky labels and nicknames. At the end of the day it's your perception of yourself that defines you, not others. It defines what you perceive to be true and too good to be true. Maybe God's love is a bit hard to take in. Maybe like us, you know God loves you but feel

> Talk to yourself like you would someone you love.
>
> -Brene Brown

He must be disappointed in you. The sin, the constant fall to earthly things, the failure to seek Him has forced you to believe God's love for you is distant and strained.

DEFINE YOURSELF AS ONE RADICALLY LOVED BY GOD. THIS IS YOUR TRUE SELF, EVERY OTHER IDENTITY IS AN ILLUSION.
-BRENNAN MANNING

I once read a statement about love that has always stuck with me. "We accept the love we think we deserve." Wow! When you hear words like these your heart can either sink or soar with their reality. When you believe God is disappointed in you, the only love you think you deserve and will accept is a disappointed, only-getting-in-by-the-skin-of-your-teeth love. A love out of obligation. However, John gives us a picture of someone whose identity had nothing to do with himself, but everything to do with Jesus' true, unconditional love for him. John is known as "the disciple whom Jesus loved."

If you read the Gospels you may think John is slightly arrogant to himself in this way, as if he believed he was the best disciple. John came to understand that nothing and no one on earth defined Jesus. The entirety of Jesus' identity came from knowing He was perfectly loved by His Father. As John walked with Jesus, he experienced Christ's unconditional love and never wanted to leave it.

I'm sure John had his names deep within himself he believed to be true. *Just a fisherman, nothing special, destined for mediocrity, forgettable...*But John learned from Jesus that nothing he did was mediocre. Nothing he saw was forgettable. John let Christ's love transform him. John lived like Jesus lived. He lived loved.

We've called you *Restless Heart* because we've been there too, but we don't want you to remain restless. When you live loved, those shameful, false core beliefs are washed

He calls me beautiful like it's my name

away and you are given a new name. John's beloved identity was not a result of never failing. When Jesus said He loved John, that was his new name; the core of his being, what he saw in himself. He was loved and that's all he ever needed to be.

Do we deserve this love? No! But Jesus freely gives it anyway. You need to know you are pursued and desired by the heart of Christ. Will you hand over who you see deep within yourself, the names you let define you, and what you think you deserve?

He paid the price for you to deserve His love. Let Christ give you the name of *His beloved.* Live loved! Love,

Expectant Heart
#madeknown

Song List -

1. *Getting into You* - Relient K
2. *When You Look at Me* - Brandon Heath
3. *Keep Me A Child* - Kings Choir
4. *Beloved* - Tenth Ave North
5. *My Delight* - Will Reagan
6. *God with Us* - Bryan and Katie Torwalt

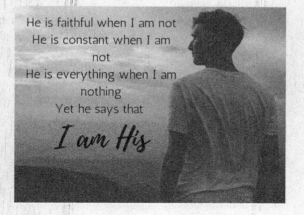

He is faithful when I am not
He is constant when I am not
He is everything when I am nothing
Yet he says that
I am His

DEAR RESTLESS HEART,
GOD MET ME MORE THAN HALFWAY,
HE FREED ME FROM MY ANXIOUS
FEARS. NEVER HIDE YOUR FEELINGS
FROM HIM. IS ANYONE CRYING FOR
HELP? GOD IS LISTENING, READY TO
RESCUE YOU. IF YOUR HEART IS BRO-
KEN, YOU'LL FIND GOD RIGHT THERE;
IF YOU'RE KICKED IN THE GUT, HE'LL
HELP YOU CATCH YOUR BREATH.

PSALM 34:4-5, 17-18

90

LOVE,
ETERNAL HEART

Eight

WAITING ON THE WORLD TO CHANGE
Thirsty for Order

Dear Restless Heart,

Details. Even in dying, He didn't miss one. From the cross, with every agonizing breath, Jesus still thought of all He needed to do for others. But He saved the best for last. Mary. His mother. Sometimes we forget Jesus' humanity. We focus so much on the fact that He was God with us that we forget He was also a human being. A perfect one, but still, a human being. His mother had felt Him grow in her belly and held Him tenderly when He nursed. She had been there for his first wobbly steps and guided His behavior as an adolescent. With each new stage, she had had to relinquish her hold on this precious firstborn.

Yes, every mom has to go through the same thing with her children, but take this mom's surrender to a whole new level. A much higher level. This mom had to take a back seat to the wishes of the Maker of heaven and earth. Her grown son had accepted His purpose in life—death.

Truly, she was Jesus' first disciple. It was a hard road, but nothing could have prepared her for what happened at Calvary. Watching Him die was horrific enough, but all those taunts screamed at Him...she could barely breathe. Her son was not oblivious. Every aspect of her life to come was on His mind even as His body was racked with searing pain. He knew how desperate her welfare could become in that first century culture. She was a widow and therefore her care was in the hands of her firstborn son, who wouldn't be around much longer. But He had a plan for her and provision.

There are moments which mark your life; moments when you realize nothing will ever be the same and time is divided into two parts: BEFORE this and AFTER this.

god whispers:
I am here *for you.*
I am *here.*
I am.

He looked at His mother who was quietly sobbing. Then He looked at His best friend, John. How sad he looked. It would bless him to be given the favor of taking care of his best friend's mom. So, pulling His body up on that nail smashed through his feet, He grabbed just enough air to speak. "John, this is your mother." Then He addressed His mother. "Woman, this is your son." He met her right where she was—brokenhearted. I believe that is why He didn't address her even as Mother, and certainly not with any motherly name He may have called her. You see, He remembered the prophesy spoken to her shortly after His earthly birth...that the spear that pierced His side would also pierce her heart.

He didn't want to make it any worse by calling her a name dear to her heart. A heart torn in two.

Mary was in a transition. Aren't they the hardest? Once you are firmly planted in a season, it gets easier, even though the change from one to the next is difficult.

"Of one thing I am perfectly sure: God's story never ends with ashes."

Elisabeth Elliot

But the Divine had had a plan all along. He had purposely picked Mary to bring the Incarnation into the world because He knew she would be obedient. She said so when the angel told her the plans, "Let it be with me just as you say" (Luke 1:38). This was certainly a game changer for Mary. We all have those moments though, in some form. A job loss, a death, a cancer diagnosis, a divorce. Life is changed forever. This story teaches us that Jesus will meet us right in our transition, with provision and a plan.

Love,
Experienced Heart

Faith is the deliberate *confidence* in the character of God whose ways you may not understand at the time.
-Oswald Chambers

Hope Point #8 – When life is in upheaval and accustomed patterns give way, God's plans and provision remain steady and His control secure.

Dear Restless Heart,

Waiting on the world to change is the perfect phrase to describe seasons of transition in which you find yourself forced to move from the warm safety of your normal life to shaky, unfamiliar ground. Mary knew this day would come from day one with Gabriel. But standing here in front of her firstborn beloved son, Jesus, tortured on a cross, it seemed her whole world was crumbling beneath her feet. Her past, now a wonderful memory. Her present, a horrifying, heartbreaking reality. And her future completely uncertain.

But of all the things Jesus could have done with some of His final words, all the wonders He could have performed, all  the words from His Father He could have spoken to prove He was the Messiah, Jesus chose to address His mother. To meet her in her heartbreak. To let her know she was safe and secure in this time of transition. And to provide her peace for the perceived chaos in her future. He gave her everything she needed to walk away from the cross that day.

In seasons of change, we fear many things; but most of all, we fear for provision in the face of uncertainty. How do we begin to walk from the safe into the unknown? Mary's journey clearly shows we cannot do so on our own strength. Yes, the cliche heard when traveling from one season to the next is, "Like a priceless masterpiece, you are being chiseled, molded, and refined to bring you closer to who God created you to be." But we think we have to suck it up, absorb all the hurt, deny all the longing for the past, and accept all the change – alone. We have somehow believed the lie that real strength comes when you prove yourself – with no one at our side to help you. As if when we bear all the weight and hardship which change brings *alone*, our faith and dependence in God will increase. Kinda silly, isn't it? All too often we think God can only do one thing at a time. Our God is bigger than that. Much bigger. He can not only mold you, chisel you, and refine you through the fires of uncertainty, but He can also walk with you in the process. Comfort you in the dark scary valleys, and provide for your needs.

97

"He's not safe. But He's good."
-C.S. Lewis

When Jesus was on the cross, He was saving all mankind. Performing the ultimate act to free humanity for the rest

of eternity, but He still saw His mother's hurt.
God is not too busy doing His work to see you in
your hurting, He cares about you in your seasons
of transition and provides for you through it, by
your side. He is doing so even if you haven't heard
His voice in what feels like eons. Jesus gave Mary
what she needed to walk away from Calvary, but
He also used her habit of storing treasures in her
heart. All throughout her life, Mary held close God's
moments of faithfulness and unbreakable promises.

Just because you may not be hearing God in this
season doesn't mean He is not still by your side.
You haven't done anything wrong to prevent you
from hearing his direction. This may just be a time
of silence. He is still working His plans, providing for
your needs. Hold tight to His promises. Just like for
His mother, His voice will come.

Love,
Expectant Heart

#madeable

Song List -

1. *You don't Miss a Thing* - Bethel Music
2. *Sparrow (Under Heavens Eyes)* - Tenth Avenue North
3. *Afloat* - Sol Rexius
4. *Good to Me* - Audrey Assad
5. *I Won't Let you Go* - Switchfoot
6. *Honey* - Kings Choir
7. *Mountain to Valley* - Bread and Wine

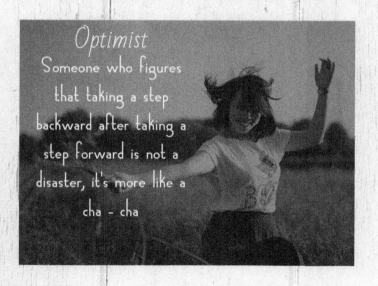

Optimist
Someone who figures that taking a step backward after taking a step forward is not a disaster, it's more like a cha - cha

DEAR RESTLESS HEART,
I ASK - ASK THE GOD OF OUR MAS-
TER, JESUS CHRIST, THE GOD OF GLO-
RY - TO MAKE YOU INTELLIGENT AND

*DISCERNING IN KNOWING HIM PER-
SONALLY, YOUR EYES FOCUSED AND
CLEAR, SO THAT YOU CAN SEE EXACT-
LY WHAT IT IS HE IS CALLING YOU
TO DO, GRASP THE IMMENSITY OF
THIS GLORIOUS WAY OF LIFE HE HAS
FOR HIS FOLLOWERS, OH, THE UTTER
EXTRAVAGANCE OF HIS WORK IN US
WHO TRUST HIM...*

EPHESIANS 1:17-19

LOVE,
ETERNAL HEART

100

Nine

NO SUCH THING
Thirsty for Clarity

Dear Restless Heart,

Conclusions. We all draw them. This event happened so this scenario must be true. Here's the circumstantial evidence, so this is what is needed. Sometimes we get it all wrong. We think facts are the same as truth. They are not. Not when you are dealing with the God of the universe. He's never been bound by earthly realities. Would this One who raised Lazarus from the dead really be captive to the grave Himself? His Truth always trumps the facts, because one plus one in His hands may equal more than two. Mary Magdalene found that to be the case early that first Easter morning.

She took spices to anoint Jesus' body for burial. He was dead, she reasoned, so His body needed attention. But she was wrong. She also drew the wrong conclusion when she looked in the tomb and no one was there. She assumed His body had been stolen. It had not. As she came out of the tomb, she saw a man. Since the tomb was in a garden, she figured he was the gardener. Incorrect again.

God is making things happen for you. Even when you don't see it, even when you don't feel it, even when it's not evident... God is working on your prayers.

Their conversation was short, but long enough to have its desired effect. Charles Haddon Spurgeon, the famous English preacher for whom my daddy and granddaddy were named, said it like this, "Jesus can preach a perfect sermon in one word." "Mary." That's all He said. But the power of that one word. Overjoyed and incredulous, Mary Magdalene held on to Him so hard and for so long that

He finally had to tell her to let Him go. He had places to go and people to see.

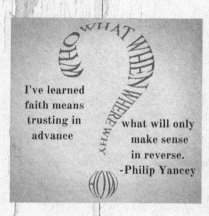

I've learned faith means trusting in advance what will only make sense in reverse.
-Philip Yancey

Mary Magdalene had come to show her last measure of devotion and honor to Jesus. She had been a faithful disciple since that amazing day when He had delivered her from seven demons. She had been the last one at the cross and the first one to the tomb. Jesus rewarded her for that. She was the first to see Him risen and would be the first to tell others.

103

Life can get confusing. We never see the big picture like Jesus does. A conversation with Jesus can clear up

I've never met a strong person with an easy past

our confusion, or at the very least, calm us down because we know every detail of the situation is in His capable hands. Regardless of the problem the answer is always to hang out with Jesus. Talking to Him makes all the difference.

Love,
Experienced Heart

Hope Point #9 – There is no fear in living God's way because there is no limit to His patience with us when we misunderstand His directions, His plans, or His next step for our lives.

Dear Restless Heart,
Do you ever go through a difficult experience, make it out the other side, look around for a second to see if you learned anything, then ask God *"Why in the world did all of that have to happen?"* It's not that you are angry with God, you just desperately want clarity. Everything seems foggy and you are

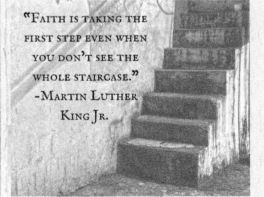

"FAITH IS TAKING THE FIRST STEP EVEN WHEN YOU DON'T SEE THE WHOLE STAIRCASE."
-MARTIN LUTHER KING JR.

left squinting down the road trying to see what might become of it.

This year I wanted nothing more than clarity and wow, that's an exhausting place to be! I went through two very hard circumstances that called me out of my comfort zone into a place of uncertainty. While I walked through them, I had no safe group of friends, no things I loved to pour myself into, and I was tired and scared, wondering if I had heard God correctly. It felt like I asked God hourly why I was in this season, what He wanted me to accomplish, and if my life would ever feel clear again. My heart was completely and utterly restless. Can you relate?

105

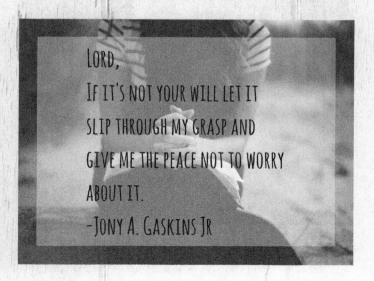

LORD,
IF IT'S NOT YOUR WILL LET IT
SLIP THROUGH MY GRASP AND
GIVE ME THE PEACE NOT TO WORRY
ABOUT IT.
-TONY A. GASKINS JR

I was sure I would have this amazing revelation by the end of the year - why God had let me go through such a hard season, but that wasn't the case. Still confused, it took a lot of time and trust for the clarity to come. It wasn't this huge unveiling either; it came like clouds clearing from a storm, gently and slowly until one day I realized why. It was so I could really understand what it's like to feel stuck and slowly sinking in hopelessness. There is no way I could have ever written a book on hope until I knew every emotion that makes a hopeless, restless heart.

When a train goes through a tunnel and it gets dark, you don't throw away the ticket and jump off. You sit still and trust the engineer.
-Corrie Ten Boom

While I was writing this book, an anonymous encourager sent me letters with quotes that lessened my fears and gave me strength to keep writing. One quote from E. L. Doctorow read, "Writing a novel is like driving a car at night. You can see only as far as your headlights, but you can make the whole trip that way." True for writing a book *and* writing the story of your life. In your season of uncertainty, you will want a full road map to understand all you are embarking on. But the Lord knows what you need more than you and His plans are more than you could imagine. All you need is the light He provides in your present circumstance, trusting in Him rather than in your own understanding. There is an end to every season and He is faithful to the end. And clear is something beautiful to behold.

> "I find that there are three levels of clarity. When I only think about something, my thoughts are embryonic and muddled. When I speak about it, my thoughts become clearer, though not always. When I write about it, I jump to a new level of clarity."
>
> ED WELCH

Love,
Expectant Heart

#madeaware

Song List -
1. *Your Hands* - JJ Heller
2. *While I'm Waiting* - John Waller
3. *Thy Will* - Hillary Scott and the Scott Family
4. *More than You Think I Am* - Danny Gokey
5. *Stay and Wait* - Hillsong UNITED
6. *One Thing* -Tenth Avenue North
7. *Time* - John Lucas

DEAR RESTLESS HEART,
BUT I'LL TAKE THE HAND OF THOSE
WHO DON'T KNOW THE WAY, WHO
CAN'T SEE WHERE THEY'RE GOING. I'LL
BE A PERSONAL GUIDE TO THEM, DI-
RECTING THEM THROUGH UNKNOWN
COUNTRY. I'LL BE RIGHT THERE TO
SHOW THEM WHAT ROADS TO TAKE,
MAKE SURE THEY DON'T FALL INTO
THE DITCH. THESE ARE THE THINGS
I'LL BE DOING FOR THEM-STICKING
WITH THEM, NOT LEAVING THEM FOR
A MINUTE.

ISAIAH 42:16-17

LOVE,
ETERNAL HEART

Ten

STOP THIS TRAIN
Thirsty for Renewal

Dear Restless Heart,
He actually said it. Those words we think but are too timid to speak because they reveal our hearts. Hearts that are in shreds. "We had hoped..." Those words confound us. What punctuation could we possibly use? We can't bear to put a period at the end of that thought. So, we put three. And the sentiment just hangs out there. The disappointment, the sigh, the need for an explanation. Is there any good news? Will there ever be renewal? That's where we are in this story.

Cleopas and a friend are walking back to their hometown, Emmaus. They had been to Jerusalem for the Passover feast. Such a joyous time for the

Jews—remembering God's deliverance from their slavery in Egypt. But then, those events they could never have imagined. Like a free fall. Tumbling, swirling, crazy. Jesus, the rabbi they had been following for three years. That same one who was hailed last week with Hosannas. Now sentenced to die on a cross by an ugly, screaming crowd. And He's dead. Dead.

Even the strongest of us have moments when the burdens of life seem too great. It's then that the Lord whispers... Come to me, all who are weary and burdened, and I will give you rest. Matthew 11:28

And these two are left with an abundance of thoughts. A jumble of words. But no understanding. So they trudge. Seven miles down dusty roads. Trying to make some sense of it. So deep in thought that they hardly notice the stranger who appears out of nowhere. Until he asks the unthinkable question, "What are you talking about?"

Are you kidding me? Where do you live? Obviously not around here. And it all spills out. The hopes, the expectations. And the sad reality. Nothing happened as it was supposed to. But then this stranger begins to speak. Beginning with Moses, and continuing through all the scriptures, He explains things in a way they had never heard or thought. How all the beyond-all-reason events of the weekend were actually right on track. What? They are mesmerized. And all of a sudden, they are back in Emmaus. So they beg him. Stay with us. Eat with us. And that's when it happens. He breaks the bread and they take it and see. It's Jesus! The Savior. How can this be? And then He's gone. And in a way, they are too. That old Cleopas and friend—never again. In an instant, everything is different. Everything. And they must tell the rest of the disciples!

> # ROCK BOTTOM
> ## BECAME THE
> ## SOLID
> ## FOUNDATION ON
> ## WHICH I REBUILT
> ## MY LIFE.
> -J.K. ROWLING

Those wearisome seven miles they had just endured, one step after the other, plodding, heavy, hard...they sprinted them back. And in their excitement the words just spilling out...He lives! Jesus lives! He walked with us and talked to us! And they were renewed. Changed. Life would never be the same. All because of a conversation with Jesus.

Love,
Experienced Heart

Hope Point #10 – When we give God our weary, strained, life-is-hard places, He refills our tank, gets us back on track, and reenergizes us for our journey.

Dear Restless Heart,

Have you ever received unexpected tragic news that left you with lost hopes in something you thought was steadfast? You desperately need to get away, but of course, some kind soul catches you and asks, "Are you ok?" Your defenses go up; you need to escape. Bad timing, right? You want to say, "Seriously? Nope, I'm not and I'd prefer not to talk about it, thank you very much!" But it's a lost battle. You can't take it another second and you break down. The whole story flows out between breathy sobs. The unexpected ending, the disappointment, the hopes left unfulfilled. Not even a spark remains of the fire that once burned so brightly inside you.

113

Get your fire back.

It's not over
until God says
it's over.

Start believing again.

START DREAMING AGAIN.

Start pursuing what
God put in your heart.

This is how Cleopas and his fellow disciple felt on the road to Emmaus after that tragic weekend. They needed to get away from Jerusalem or they would crumple in a heap. As the two conversed, a kind stranger walked up and asked what they were talking about. Bad timing. Their hearts drop. They froze. They have just lost their best friend. But the walls go up; they don't want to tell the whole story. They just want to escape. *Are you serious? How don't you know all that has happened this weekend?* But then Jesus in disguise kindly asks, "What things?" The walls break. The two disciples tell Him everything. All that happened to Jesus, their crushed hopes, their weariness. Everything.

On the road to Emmaus we see such a clear picture of the heart of Christ. He kept the disciples from recognizing Him just to *be* with them, to hear their sorrow. Jesus never forces Himself on us. He knows what pain and heartbreak feel like. He knows there is a time to mourn and tenderly walks with us along that way. He listens and comforts us. Doesn't rush, just listens and empathizes. He lets them process their heartache and questions, not forcing the answers on them.

When you take time with God and listen to His voice, He renews your strength and enables you to handle life.

Ever notice sometimes after you're able to process your situation in those so-called "bad timing" moments, that all that you let out makes room for healing to enter in? Jesus let the disciples process what was on their hearts. He then filled in the empty spaces with the truth of His identity and the authority and wisdom He had. The chaotic events of the weekend began to make sense. For the first time in days, their hearts beat again and they begged Him to stay. Then, in an act so intimate and familiar, Jesus broke bread with them. Their eyes were opened and for that moment Jesus stood before them again.

"Did not our hearts burn within us?" was their response. Did you know Emmaus means *hot springs used for healing?* Cleopas and his friend had lost their spark and passion; they were thirsty for renewal. They experienced it as they walked with Jesus. His words were like warm, healing water, bringing hope and restoration. The fire was gone but the embers were still burning deep within. Jesus relit that passion as He revealed He was alive. He can bring renewal out of the deepest turmoil. What seemed to be a poorly timed conversation in a weary moment turned out to be God's perfect timing, bringing renewal and passion.

He is the God of immeasurably more, the God of new things, the God of umpteenth chances and incredible plans.

And He loves you

Where have you lost hope? Have you shared those disappointments with Jesus? He is ready to walk with you as you process and bring renewal and healing where all hope has been lost. All it takes is a conversation.

Love,
Expectant Heart

#madewhole

Song List -
1. *In Your Presence* - Elevation Worship
2. *Busted Heart* - for King & Country
3. *Let us Adore* - Elevation Worship
4. *Healing Begins* - Tenth Avenue North
5. *God Alone (Psalm 62)* - Will Reagan
6. *Worn* - Tenth Avenue North
7. *God is No Stranger (feat. Paul Zach)* - Joseph Holm

DEAR RESTLESS HEART,
TRUST GOD FROM THE BOTTOM OF YOUR HEART; DON'T TRY TO FIGURE OUT EVERYTHING ON YOUR OWN. LISTEN FOR GOD'S VOICE IN EVERYTHING

YOU DO, EVERYWHERE YOU GO; HE'S THE ONE WHO WILL KEEP YOU ON TRACK.

PROVERBS 3:5-8

LOVE,
ETERNAL HEART

118

Eleven

BOLD AS LOVE
Thirsty for Courage

Dear Restless Heart,

The disciples got many things wrong about Jesus, but they got the most important thing right; they let His voice override all other voices. And I'm sure there were plenty of those voices after the Crucifixion. Scary voices. Run-and-hide voices. So, these disciples, these young men barely out of their teens or early twenties, did just that. They ran and hid. Behind closed doors. But in one supernatural moment, Jesus taught them two vital lessons they would never forget. Lessons about fear and their reactions to it. First, locked doors still don't bring peace. Second, locked doors won't keep out the Savior. He walked through that locked door... through it, like it was flung wide open. And then

He spoke the words those frightened followers needed to hear, "Peace to you."

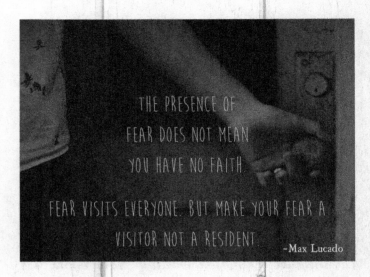

THE PRESENCE OF
FEAR DOES NOT MEAN
YOU HAVE NO FAITH.

FEAR VISITS EVERYONE. BUT MAKE YOUR FEAR A
VISITOR NOT A RESIDENT.
                                            -Max Lucado

120

When I get scared, it always boils down to the same two mistakes: listening to the wrong voices and asking the wrong questions. There are two voices which try to scream their message above the quiet whisper of God—the devil and the world. Now, I can easily distinguish the voice of Satan versus my Savior. Jesus' voice is always calming, empowering and kind. Satan's is upsetting, demoralizing, and mean. His timing is so predictable too; when the sun goes down, or when I am alone, weary or angry, I know I can expect to hear from him. He is the ultimate opportunist.

God	Satan
Stills you	Rushes you
Reassures you	Frightens you
Leads you	Pushes you
Enlightens you	Confuses you
Forgives you	Condemns you
Encourages you	Discourages you
Calms you	Stresses you
Comforts you	Worries you

The other voice that throws me off track and makes me afraid is the voice of the world. This messenger is not quite so easy to recognize because its banter is everywhere. When my focus is clearly on my problem, my need, and my lack, then I know I need to question my thinking and my hearing. Usually I have allowed the small-g-god to take the place of my all-caps-GOD. I've listened to the world's opinion and forgotten that Christ is the Victor, regardless of the battle. Nothing, nothing surprises, overwhelms, or knocks Him off His throne.

Asking the wrong questions. This lesson takes a lifetime to learn, but every step in the right direction is a good thing, so don't forsake this discipline. Here's the gist. It's a tiny word. An unnoticed word. Only three letters. But how they are arranged makes all the difference in our hearts and lives. The letters of the word are o, h, and w. Our tendency is to place them in this order: how. How? It is always followed by a question mark. We want understanding. All the time. It is the characteristic of the finite to long for comprehension of the infinite.

We ask God, "How?" We're disappointed when He rearranges those letters in His response. He answers us all too often with "Who". Rather than unpacking the scenar-

Doubt kills more dreams than failure ever will

io with all the details, He tells us our companion on the journey. At the end of Jesus' time on earth, after He commissioned His disciples to go, baptize, and teach in His Name, He didn't explain how this would all happen. He told them He would be with them. "I'll be with you as you do this, day after day after day, right up to the end of the age" (Matthew 28:20). No how, just Who. In our questions and fears, He'll do the same for us. Lord, teach us to let that be enough.

Love,
Experienced Heart

Hope Point #11 – God understands that telling us how life will unfold will not give us the peace we need nearly as much as telling us Who will accompany us.

Courage Dear Heart

-C.S. Lewis

Dear Restless Heart, We all love a good underdog story – when those with every odd against them finally find their victory. My favorite is the incredible story of the 1980 US Olympic hockey team portrayed in the Disney movie *Miracle*. Combine the great acting of Kurt Russell with my borderline unhealthy obsession with the Olympics, and you've got a Chloe Grabeman special! I saw it in the movie theater when I was eight years old, and probably another forty times since then. But I still clinch a pillow to the point of feathers exploding in the final seconds of that historic point made against the Soviet Union team. The miracle on ice.

"It's impossible." said Pride.

"It's risky." said Experience.

"It's pointless." said Reason.

"Give it a try," whispered the Heart.

There's a reason we love underdog stories so much: their determination, belief, and courage are greater than their fear. There's a quote in *Miracle* that captures the underdog psyche. Coach Herb Brooks shouts, "The name on the front of the jersey is way more important than the name on the back." Wow, that's true as well for us, in having the courage to live out our calling. The name on the

124

front of your jersey - the cause you are fighting for, living for God, living the life He calls you to, is much more important than your name on the back, or your fear of failing.

WHAT WOULD
LIFE BE LIKE IF
WE HAD NO
COURAGE TO
ATTEMPT
ANYTHING?
-VINCENT VAN GOGH

125

The disciples were the best rag tag underdog team there ever was, but on that day, locked in the upper room, they felt utterly defeated. They were without a leader, hiding for their lives. But despite the reality of death and the locked doors, Jesus appeared among them. Of all the things Jesus could have said, He chose to speak to that uncontrollable fear raging within their hearts. "Peace," was all He said. Proving His victory over the ultimate battle, death, Jesus invited them to step into their calling with His promise never to leave them.

Again, in *Miracle*, Coach Brooks exclaims, "This cannot be a team of common men, because common men go nowhere. You have to be uncommon." The disciples were as common as they come, a bunch of fishermen. They felt fear and they doubted their abilities. They knew their purpose. It was now time to walk it out. What if fear had kept them behind those locked doors? We wouldn't have the gospel! The disciples found the courage to walk out their calling. That courage was not in themselves, but in the peace and power of Jesus and His constant presence with them. He was their cause, their courage, and their strength. Period. We have that same power living inside of us.

Don't be afraid to try something new. Amateurs built the ark. Professionals built the Titanic.

We love underdogs because they inspire us and give us the chance to believe in impossibilities. Think of the people who have impacted and inspired you. What if they hadn't had the courage to take the steps that led them to you? Your life would be completely different.

LIVING BY
FAITH
INCLUDES THE
CALL TO
SOMETHING
GREATER
THAN
COWARDLY
SELF
PRESERVATION

-J.R.R. TOLKIN

If you courageously walk out your calling, your life will impact others just as dramatically and give just as much meaning and inspiration as those who inspired you. Inward insecurities and outward opposition are always elements in the underdog story. But there is a battle to be fought. When fear tries to keep you from moving, let Jesus in. Ask Him to speak peace over your worried heart; ask Him for the courage to pick up your sword again. God will use your journey to forever impact lives

127

around you. Have the courage to live for the front of your jersey.

Love,
Expectant Heart

#madefearless

"Everything around us that we call life was made by people who are no smarter than you. And you can build your own things, you can build your own life that people can live in."
-Ashton Kutcher

Song List -
1. *Strong Enough* - Matthew West
2. *Life is Beautiful* - The Afters
3. *Give us your Courage* - Tim Hughes
4. *Take Heart* - Hillsong United

5. *Glorious Ruins* – Hillsong Worship
6. *Banner of Love* – Luminate
7. *Fearlessly* – Luminate
8. *Voice of Truth* – Casting Crowns

"it had long since come to my attention that people of accomplishments rarely sat back and let things happen to them. they went out and happened to things."

—leonardo da vinci

DEAR RESTLESS HEART,
KEEP YOUR EYES ON JESUS, WHO
BOTH BEGAN AND FINISHED THIS
RACE WE'RE IN. STUDY HOW HE DID
IT. BECAUSE HE NEVER LOST SIGHT OF
WHERE HE WAS HEADED-THAT EXHIL-
ARATING FINISH IN AND WITH GOD-
HE COULD PUT UP WITH ANYTHING
ALONG THE WAY: THE CROSS, SHAME,
WHATEVER. AND NOW HE'S THERE IN
THE PLACE OF HONOR, RIGHT ALONG-
SIDE GOD. WHEN YOU FIND YOURSELF
FLAGGING IN YOUR FAITH, GO OVER
THAT STORY AGAIN...THAT WILL SHOOT
ADRENALINE INTO YOUR SOULS!

HEBREWS 12:2-3

LOVE,
ETERNAL HEART

Twelve

BIGGER THAN MY BODY
Thirsty for Purpose

Dear Restless Heart,

Being a leaky bucket is not always negative. I read a Chinese proverb recently that I joyfully want to "Christian-ize." A young boy drew water from a well every day, carrying two buckets on a bamboo pole slung across his shoulders. One bucket was perfect; the other had a few holes in it. Each day as he reached his destination, the leaky bucket was only half full. This made the leaky bucket sad. One day, it got up the courage to apologize for its imperfections. The boy quietly nodded his head, filled both buckets and began his trek home. On the road, the leaky bucket was very quiet, humiliated, and heartbroken. But as they walked, the boy pointed to each side of the path. The perfect bucket side was covered only in bare dirt. The leaky bucket side had grass and even a flower or two poking through, all because it had been "accidentally" watered from the holes in the leaky bucket. The landscape had been changed simply because of the bucket's imperfections.

How often I wish I were perfect. But perfect brings no healing or encouragement to anyone else, only guilt. Being real, even leaky, is infinitely useful in God's hands. Sometimes our hardest lessons, trials, or imperfections end up as our greatest tools for ministry. We water our human environment through the holes in our bucket.

Many years ago, I took a test to show my spiritual gifts. I wanted the test to show my great abilities as a teacher—a teacher of the Bible. But try as I may, the results didn't show that. They revealed my tendencies and ability to give encouragement. I didn't like those test results, and I told God plainly. I said, "Really, God? That's the best gift You could give me? I think that's a stupid gift!"

The place where God calls you to is the place where your deepest gladness and the world's deepest hunger meet.

-Frederick Buechner

Decades later, I embrace my gift of encouragement. Embrace it. Why? Because through hard times with gravely ill children and then my own cancer, I have been the recipient of encouragement in all its forms — calls, cards, rides, food, flowers, prayers—and

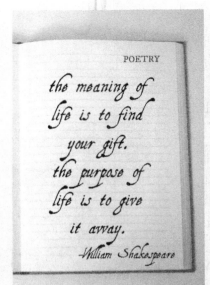

POETRY

*the meaning of
life is to find
your gift.
the purpose of
life is to give
it away.*

-William Shakespeare

I know beyond the shadow of a doubt that they make a difference. I now understand how the leaks in my bucket can water others too. I regularly counsel women facing mastectomies after having two myself. God knew what He was doing when He combined my imperfections with my gifting. He has just as perfectly knit your imperfections and gifting together. Please embrace them with more grace than I did many years ago!

God perfectly understands the power of story. Have you ever taken the time to think out your one-of-a-kind God-story that only you can tell? Spoken by the one who actually lived it, it is fresh, alive, and life-giving. There are people for whom only your story will make a difference. Add on your own particular style and capabilities and you've discovered your unique formula that will refresh and water this hurting world, one person at a time. So, don't try to be a perfect bucket. Be that extraordinarily real, leaky bucket, ready to bring encouragement in the wonderfully wacky way God has given to you. Only as you begin to embrace that unique calling will you realize just how desperately thirsty the world is for it.

Love,
Experienced Heart

Tell me, what is it you plan to do with your one wild and precious life?

Hope Point #12 – Following God's unique plan for our lives using our God-given abilities, passions, and imperfections brings joy to us as it meets the needs of others.

Dear Restless Heart,
Nothing can make you more restless than not knowing what you should be doing. Surrounded by

others who have seemed to find their purpose and passion in life, you wonder if you've taken a wrong turn. If you have anything beautiful and different to offer the world. If it will ever be your time. You constantly ask God how to find your fire in life, but the answers don't often come clearly. When we get restless, we get reckless. Ever thought something like this: *Ok, I've sought God and wise council. They didn't help much. I need to take this in my own hands. I can't just continue to wait and do nothing. Every day that goes by is more wasted time for me to do what I was meant to do.*

136

This was how I felt through much of college. For all of my freshman year I didn't have a major, and that was constantly on my mind. I felt as if I were already behind in my education and what I wanted to do with my life. I

> **If you think you've blown God's plan for your life, rest in this. You, my beautiful friend, are not that powerful.**
> Lisa Bevere

felt useless...and scared of a life of uselessness. I thought my parents' money was going to waste and I was afraid I would never find something in this world that would give me joy.

Having an expectant heart doesn't mean God is going to show you everything He wants you to do all at once or even when you ask Him desperately in prayer. Expectancy comes when you know He is working even when you can't see which way to go or hear any direction from His voice.

The only way I can describe it is this way. I have a friend who is an artist and creates in a very powerful and unique way. He stands in front of a huge black canvas, ready to create a masterpiece, turns on music, and immediately begins to paint random brush strokes all over the canvas in various art mediums. His audience sits captivated, trying to figure out what he's creating. But it's impossible. Not until the end does he add one final brushstroke or flip the entire canvas upside down to reveal the beautiful subject. The black canvas, the music, the different colors, and all the seemingly random brush strokes aren't random at all. Every part of the performance serves a purpose in creating the final product.

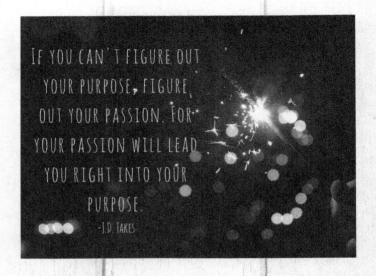

IF YOU CAN'T FIGURE OUT
YOUR PURPOSE, FIGURE
OUT YOUR PASSION. FOR
YOUR PASSION WILL LEAD
YOU RIGHT INTO YOUR
PURPOSE.
-J.D. JAKES

God created you with gifts and experiences that will be revealed along the way to fill a need in the world only you can fill as you live a life reflecting the hope you have found in your unique life in Christ. Your story, your struggles, and your gifts might be the only way someone else can connect with and experience God.

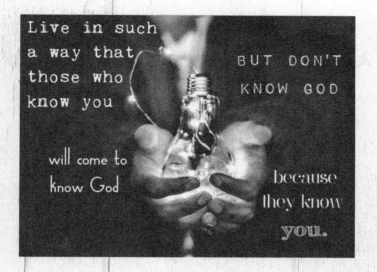

Live in such a way that those who know you will come to know God BUT DON'T KNOW GOD because they know you.

You don't need to take matters into your own hands; you can wait expectantly, captivated by knowing that all the little things about you are being used. In this position, you are ready to see all the countless blessings easily missed when you focus so stubbornly on the one thing God is not doing. Some days pass without knowing what you are doing next, but one little thing can happen and the vision you have been so desiring might come into full view. Every dab of paint along the way then makes sense and you see He's been working the whole time. I encourage you to give your dreams and desires to God and watch how He gives them back abundantly!

Love,
Expectant Heart

#madeexpectant

Song List -
1. *Stay and Wait* - Hillsong United
2. *Tapestry* - Hillsong United
3. *Glorious* - Colony House
4. *Five Foot Three* - Flannel Graph
5. *Waiting for my Time to Come* - Colony House
6. *Your Promises* - Elevation Worship
7. *Shepherd of My Soul* - Rivers and Robots
8. *My Delight* - Will Reagan
9. *Architecture* - Jonathan Thulin

JESUS will take you places you never IMAGINED, but they will rarely look like what you had PLANNED.

Do you seriously think God can't use you?

Noah was a drunk

Abraham was old

Isaac was a daydreamer

DAVID HAD AN AFFAIR

Jacob was a cheater

Jonah ran from God

Paul was a murderer

Martha was a worrier

Thomas was a doubter

LAZARUS WAS DEAD

141

DEAR RESTLESS HEART,
GOD CAN DO ANYTHING YOU KNOW—
FAR MORE THAN YOU COULD EVER
IMAGINE OR GUESS OR REQUEST IN
YOUR WILDEST DREAMS! HE DOES IT
NOT BY PUSHING US AROUND BUT
BY WORKING WITHIN US, HIS SPIR-
IT DEEPLY AND GENTLY WITHIN US.
IN LIGHT OF ALL THIS, HERE'S WHAT
I WANT YOU TO DO...I WANT YOU TO

GET OUT THERE AND WALK-BETTER
YET, RUN!-ON THE ROAD GOD CALLED
YOU TO TRAVEL. BUT THAT DOESN'T
MEAN YOU SHOULD ALL LOOK AND
SPEAK AND ACT THE SAME. OUT OF
THE GENEROSITY OF CHRIST, EACH
OF US IS GIVEN HIS OWN GIFT.

EPHESIANS 3:20, 4:1-2, 7

LOVE,
ETERNAL HEART

142

Thirteen

NEON
Thirsty for ~~Quiet~~

Dear Restless Heart,

Sometimes you just need to know you're not alone,
because this crazy world can make you feel dread-
fully companionless, detached, and without hope.
Have you noticed that simply the everyday business
of living can disorient you? And that it happens so
unconsciously? It's a "Too busy for my quiet time
today, Lord," one day, and a "I'm sorry I've been
so busy, Jesus," another, and suddenly, you don't
know, or like, where you are—alone, weary, and
confused.

We have all felt the fatigue and frustration of a worn-down-to-the-bone soul. When I am either ready to drop or to explode, I know it is past time to be refilled. And no one does that like Jesus. He draws me away from the rat race to the real, the important, the eternal. Time with Him, just the two of us, gives me the space and safety to cry, vent (aloud or on paper), or just be quiet with the One who knows, understands, and helps. Sometimes I spread myself too thin or try to do too much. I am awed by the pattern Jesus lived. In His final prayer with the disciples, He said He had gotten everything done that His Father had told Him to do. He left nothing out; regretted nothing. I can't imagine! On my craziest can't-get-it-all-done days, I am prone to pick up my pace even more, when what I really need is do is slow down, be still, and rest in His presence.

You have done *Enough* today, you can rest now.

I found the most wonderful detail in a well-hidden verse in the Old Testament. First Kings 7:21 says, "He set the pillars up in the entrance porch to The Temple; the pillar to the south he named Security (Jachin) and the pillar to the north Stability (Boaz)." Here's what struck me about this verse. First, who names pillars? Obviously, God does when He wants to make a crucial point. Second, Security and Stability... aren't those the very things we long for in our lives? Hmmm. In First Kings, chapter six, it says that all the work to chisel, form, and refine these pillars was done off-site, not on the grounds of the Temple. Those pillars were placed in the Temple in silence.

As New Testament believers, we are the Temple of God. Where is the place we find our security and stability? In our quiet times. When we get busy and frazzled, Jesus waits for our cry, for our focus to turn back to Him. Often, He waits a while. He won't scream over the noise in our lives. So, my often-repeated prayer is, Lord, show me those activities that make my life loud and uneasy. And wherever I have gotten accustomed to that turbulence, forgive me and redirect me to Your quiet place of stability and security. Just as Your Father ordered Your days, order my days, Jesus. Order them to You... First. Always.

Love,
Experienced
Heart

Prayer trumps panic. Every Time.

146

Hope Point #13 – *God's presence is the listening ear for our hearts, the settling voice for our souls, and the quiet place for our spirits, reminding us what is real and necessary and eternal.*

Dear Restless Heart,
Ever feel like you have an endless to-do list, no matter where you look? Even with God? Well I get it, and it stinks to feel that way! You are exhausted and in desperate need of rest, but the to-do list shouts so loudly, you cannot escape even to God to find quiet.

Beware the barrenness of a busy
life.
-Socrates

147

You look at others and feel like your faith, knowledge of God, and desire to be with Him is lacking. You obviously need to read more books, listen to more sermons, or have this new expanse of knowledge before you deserve any rest from Him. So, you put off approaching Him until you complete these signs of devotion. Before long, you feel guilted into spending time with Him and are utterly exhausted, but feel like you don't deserve to have rest.

"Are you tired? Worn out? Burned out on religion? Come to me. Get away with me and you'll recover your life. I'll show you how to take a real rest. Walk with me and work with me - watch how I do it. Learn the unforced rhythms of grace. I won't lay anything heavy or ill-fitting on you. Keep company with me and you'll learn to live freely and lightly" (Matthew 11:28).

Busy is a choice
Stress is a choice
Joy is a choice
Choose Well

—Ann Voskamp

One of the most beautiful parts of this verse, in my opinion, is *who* Jesus addresses in His invitation.

It's not those who seem to have it together. Not those who have not fallen to temptations. No, He invites those who are weary, who have heavy, deep burdens, who can hardly take another step. He invites *you.* There is no prerequisite to come and stay. He says to take His yoke and learn from Him. His yoke is easy and His burden light. He is gentle and humble at heart, and you will find rest for your soul. Ah, exhale.

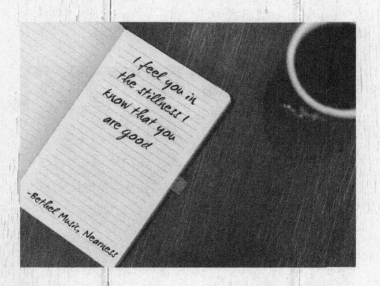

I feel you in the stillness I know that you are good

-Bethel Music, Nearness

So how have we come to believe Jesus' restful, quiet circle has an entrance fee? We often forget that Jesus is not only our Savior but also our Friend. Whenever you are overwhelmed by stress, sadness, or fear, who do you go to for help and comfort? Your best friends, right? You know you don't need to bring a huge fruit basket or study up on their life stories for them to be there for you. No! You just say you need them and they are gladly there. Everything else would be such a stupid waste of time. They love you, they know you, they want to help you - with nothing required. So why don't we treat God like this? Why can't we trust that God really is who He says He is - a Friend, a Comforter, and a place of rest?

the greatest weapon against stress is the ability to choose one thought over another
-William Jones

Knowing about someone does not make that person a close companion. You can know all about someone but still never know them. Only by spending time with someone, learning from them, does a deep relationship form. You know the sound of their voice. Their character. What they love. This is what Jesus intends for us in His invitation to rest. He loves like a Friend, with nothing required.

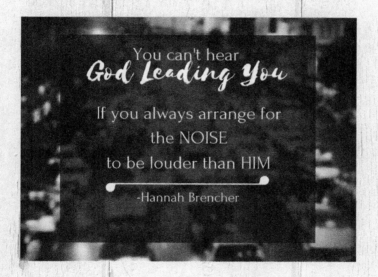

You can't hear
God Leading You
If you always arrange for
the NOISE
to be louder than HIM

-Hannah Brencher

It may come as a shock, but God does not need you. Why would God need you to read more, do more, or *be* more to be with Him? He isn't dependent on you at all. Your works don't cause Him any gain. He just wants to be with you. He is inviting you to Himself, no strings attached, so you can know Him, like the closest friend you will ever have. To know the sound of His kind, encouraging voice. To learn of His character. Nothing to cause you to compare or feel guilty; you'll find that's not His way. But rather you will find quiet in Him. You'll learn how to silence the noise.

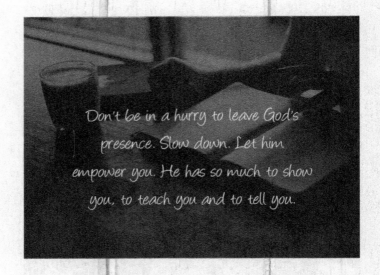

Don't be in a hurry to leave God's presence. Slow down. Let him empower you. He has so much to show you, to teach you and to tell you.

No need, either, for extensive faith to add to the to-do list. He longs for you to know Him - outside the studies, the works, and even your Bible, in a beautiful response to His goodness. Allow yourself to be quiet and rest. Come to Him and learn from Him like a friend. Join the conversation and find rest for your soul.

Love,
Expectant Heart

Song List –
1. *I Confess* – Tenth Avenue North
2. *Control (Somehow you want me)* - Tenth Avenue North
3. *Running in Circles (feat. Will Reagan)* – United Pursuit, Will Reagan
4. *Restless* – Audrey Assad
5. *Abide* – Housefires
6. *Voices* - Joseph Holm
7. *The Wick* – Housefires

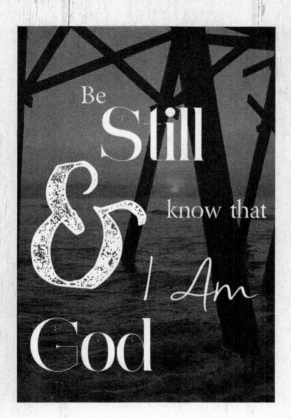

DEAR RESTLESS HEART,
HERE'S WHAT I WANT YOU TO DO: FIND A QUIET, SECLUDED PLACE SO YOU WON'T BE TEMPTED TO ROLE-PLAY BEFORE GOD. JUST BE THERE AS SIMPLY AND HONESTLY AS YOU CAN MANAGE. THE FOCUS WILL SHIFT FROM YOU TO GOD, AND YOU WILL BEGIN TO SENSE HIS GRACE.

MATTHEW 6:6

LOVE,
ETERNAL HEART

Fourteen

THE ICING ON THE CAKE
So Now What?

Dear Renewed Heart,

We can't call you Restless Heart anymore! We've tried to be faithful to the call on our book from none other than Eternal Heart: Tell them that I love them. We hope that you have met this relentless Lover of your souls in every chapter of Real and True. We long to hear that you have experienced His overwhelming grace that changes, heals, and restores, meeting you right where you are, but not leaving you there.

She is not broken anymore,

she is stronger, wiser, and more beautiful than before because God took her broken pieces and made her new again.

So now what? Continue your conversations with God. Don't ever let them stop. Read His word and become a part of His Church—one that preaches, teaches, and reaches out to the world with His truth, grace, and love. And would you do us a huge favor? Let us know how God has changed your restless heart into a settled one, sure of His promises, led by His Spirit. We'd love to hear from you at www.realandtruehope.com.

Love,
Experienced Heart

Dear Renewed Heart,

You have taken quite a journey from restless to renewed through the work of the most important heart in our little trio - Eternal Heart. Our hope is that you have come to know His heart, His thoughts, and His unrelenting love for you. Through this journey, you no longer see life with God as something you have to strive so hard for. Instead, you see a loving Father who wants to spend time with you, form a relationship, and meet you at your present moment, no matter how messy. He cares to settle your restless heart more than you could ever imagine and longs to fight your tiresome battles.

So where do we go from here, dear friend? It's time you start learning to hear and recognize His voice more clearly. Like all relationships, this one requires time and effort. Not in a way that causes you to be someone you are not, but in a way that is a constant, comfortable conversation, learning His word and talking to Him throughout your day. Tell Him the little things you don't think matter as well as the big ones and you will see His loving kindness shine through in ways you never knew pos- sible. Surround yourself with people who encourage you, challenge you, and pour into your faith. There will be mountains and valleys on your journey, but whatever your circumstances, we pray you know without any doubt that your Lord loves you and is always by your side. This hope is the real and true anchor for your soul.

Love,
Expectant Heart

DEAR RENEWED HEART,
"YOU'RE NOT IN THIS ALONE...I WANT YOU WOVEN INTO A TAPESTRY OF LOVE, IN TOUCH WITH EVERYTHING THERE IS TO KNOW OF GOD. THEN YOU WILL HAVE MINDS CONFIDENT AND AT REST, FOCUSED ON CHRIST, GOD'S GREAT MYSTERY. ALL THE RICHEST TREASURES OF WISDOM AND KNOWLEDGE ARE EMBEDDED IN THAT MYSTERY AND NOWHERE ELSE. MY COUNSEL FOR YOU IS SIMPLE AND STRAIGHTFORWARD: JUST GO AHEAD WITH WHAT YOU'VE BEEN GIVEN. YOU

RECEIVED CHRIST JESUS, THE MAS-
TER; NOW LIVE HIM."

COLOSSIANS 2:1-3, 6

LOVE,
ETERNAL HEART

Fifteen

AWESOME CHEAT SHEET
Dog-Ear this Page

HOPE POINT #1 – *What is This Hope Thing?*
There is more to this life than you ever imagined...more joy, more meaning, more hope... and it is all being offered to you.

HOPE POINT #2 – *Thirsty for Perfection*
Regardless of where you are or what you've done, God's relentlessly kind heart loves you without measure, without change, and without end.

HOPE POINT #3 – *Thirsty for Change*
God has done the unimaginable by sending Jesus to renew the conversation that was ended, reclaim us as His own, and restore our broken lives.

HOPE POINT #4 - *Thirsty for Salvation*

Jesus did what we could never do—live a perfect life, bringing us a perfect salvation, all because of His amazing grace, mercy, and love.

HOPE POINT #5 – *Thirsty for Belief*

God loves to prove Himself to us when we are honest about our doubts, questions, and misunderstandings.

163

HOPE POINT #6 - Thirsty for Forgiveness

God's love for us is based not on who we are but on who He is: overwhelmingly
gentle, undeniably good, and overflowing with grace.

164

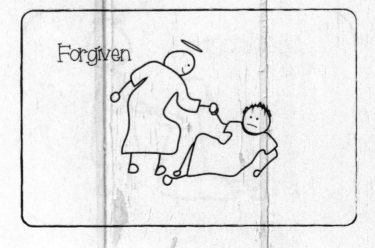

HOPE POINT #7 - Thirsty for Love and Identity

With God, our identity is always secure and we always know where we stand. We are His and we are loved.

HOPE POINT #8 – *Thirsty for Order*

166

The amazing thing about trusting God's agenda for our lives is that while He is preparing His plans for us, He is also preparing us for His plans.

HOPE POINT #9 – Thirsty for Clarity

There is no fear in living God's way because there is no limit to His patience when we misunderstand His directions, His plans, or His next step for our lives.

HOPE POINT #10 - *Thirsty for Renewal*

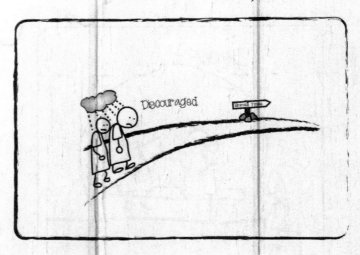

When we give God our weary, strained, life-is-hard places, He refills our tank, gets us back on track, and reenergizes us for our journeys.

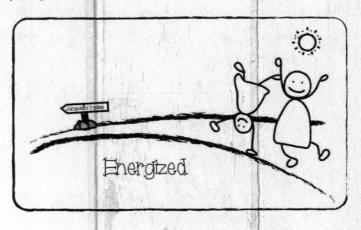

HOPE POINT #11 - *Thirsty for Courage*

God understands that telling us how life will unfold does not give us the peace we need nearly as much as telling us Who will accompany us.

169

HOPE POINT #12 – *Thirsty for Purpose*

Our God-given abilities and callings are meant to simultaneously meet the needs of others, bring us joy, and glorify God in the most natural yet passionate way.

HOPE POINT #13 – *Thirsty for Quiet*

God's presence is the listening ear for our hearts, the settling voice for our souls, and the quiet place for our spirits, reminding us what is real and necessary and eternal.

Sixteen

IN CASE YOU WANT TO KNOW
Conversations

CONVERSATION ONE – *The Thief* –
LUKE 23:40-43

CONVERSATION TWO – *Thomas* –
JOHN 20:24-29

CONVERSATION THREE – *Peter* –
MARK 16:7; LUKE 22:31-34, 22:54-62,
24:34; FIRST CORINTHIANS 15:5

CONVERSATION FOUR – *John* –
JOHN 13:23, 19:26, 20:2, 21:7, 21:20, 21:24
MARK 3:16-17; LUKE 9:54

CONVERSATION FIVE – *Mary* –
JOHN 19:25-27

CONVERSATION SIX – *Mary Magdalene* –
JOHN 20:1-18

CONVERSATION SEVEN – *Cleopas* –
MARK 16:12-13; LUKE 24:13-35

CONVERSATION EIGHT – *Disciples* –
ACTS 4:29-31

Seventeen

ADORED BOOKS:

Influential for Us, Suggested for You

These books highly impacted our lives and we think you would enjoy them too.

1. Any book by Thaddeus Rockwell Barnum, but most recently: *Real Identity; Real Love; Real Mercy; Real Courage*
2. Any book by Jennifer Kennedy Dean, but especially *Live a Praying Life: The Power of Small*
3. River Jordan – *Praying for Strangers*
4. Robert J. Morgan – *The Red Sea Rules*
5. Mark Batterson – *In a Pit with a Lion on a Snowy Day*
6. Bill Thrall and Bruce McNicol – *Truefaced*
7. Any book by Max Lucado

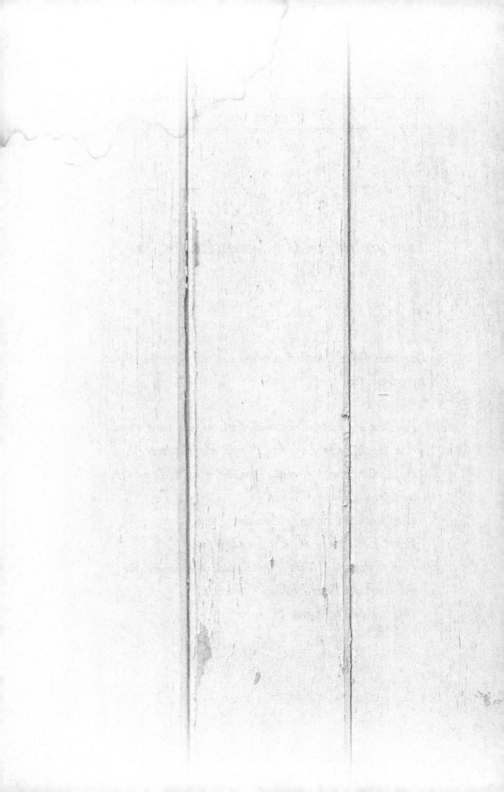

Eighteen

AND WE HAVE TO THANK
Couldn't Have Done It Without...

In one way, writing a book occurs in seclusion—all that pondering, researching, and putting pen to paper. But in other ways it is such a collaborative effort. We must give grateful mention to all who, without their help, this book would have been so much less.

Janet Rockey – Thank you for trusting me to give the Easter sunrise service at DeBordieu in 2015. God birthed this book that hallelujah morning!

Thad and Erilynne Barnum – The list is so long...friendship, mentoring, intercession! Your insightful and encouraging input blessed and empowered us.

Carolyn Byrd – How many years have you spoken life into both of our lives and over our artistic endeavors? How you bless us!

Professor Mark Vermilion – Thank you for your constant encouragement and obedience to follow God's voice. I can honestly say my life would look very different without your wise words and kindness to see what I sometimes can't see in myself. Thank you for choosing to always live for eternity.

Dr. Michael Smith – The lessons Chloe learned in your PR Writing course had such an impact on our book. God is in the details, and that class came at the perfect time.

Lee Ann Tarducci – You are a computer whiz, girl! Your ever-patient help and the joy of your infectious giggle at my repeated mistakes saved my sanity more times than I can count.

Lisa Schneider – How could one photo session be that much fun? Thank you for the laughter, the beautiful pictures, and the kind words.

The Local Grind Coffee House and Cafe – So many chapters of Real and True were scratched out over a cup of coffee or tea at your cute shop. Thanks for hosting our photo shoot too!

Jordan Clarke – Your pictures for our salvation chapter bring such clarity and urgency to our written words. Thank you.

Marsha Baker (Blessinks) – Your whimsical figures bring our Hope Points to life! Thank you for being our awesome long-distance artistic team member.

Anna Floit of The Peacock Quill – Your editing preserved each of our writing styles even as you polished our words ever so gently until they shone. We are both so grateful.

Lindsey Hartz – Your excitement and vision fills our hearts with expectation as you build our launch team. We can't wait!

Harriet Hunter – Your love, encouragement, and insightful savoring of our words brought us both such joy.

Redemption Press – As always, such a pleasure and a blessing to work with your excellent team.

Sally Keyser – You call me your teacher, but so often I am your pupil, learning the qualities of a real and true friend from you. What a joy to watch your journey as a true Jesus-follower.

Cindy Jolly – Before long, your written words will bless the world just as your spoken words and witness do right now. I am anxiously awaiting that day, my friend!

Lynn O'Meara, Elizabeth Ball, Tricia Sisney, Gloria and Petesey Reynolds, Susan White and all our other precious prayer partners – Your intercessions empowered us, revived us, and fueled our passion for each and every reader of Real and True. You are the foundation of this endeavor.

Visit Chloe and I at www.realandtruehope.com!
We'd love to hear how Real and True touched your heart!

Nineteen

BIOGRAPHY

Linda Grabeman loves to encourage people right where they are. She understands that life can get hard. After her own cancer journey, she wrote a devotional for women walking through cancer called *No Prissy Shoes: Trusting God to Walk You Through Your Cancer Journey.* She believes that no matter what, there is always a reason to give thanks, and to prove that, she wrote *Praise on Purpose: 365 Days of Uplifting Words.* So, whether you are having a hard day, a good day or a lost-your-way day, she has something perfect for you to read.

Chloe Grabeman is an unexpected author, amazed at how God has put the passion in her heart of inspiring others through words. She believes the purest of art can be found in the combination of communication and creativity. She loves to laugh until her stomach hurts and is inspired by finding God moving in the simple and unlikely places. She has a blog called "Dear Restless Heart" on their website, realandtruehope.com which focuses on trusting God with "the process", having an open mind to His good but mysterious ways.

ORDER INFORMATION

REDEMPTION
PRESS

To order additional copies of this book, please visit
www.redemption-press.com.
Also available on Amazon.com and BarnesandNoble.com
Or by calling toll free 1-844-2REDEEM.

CPSIA information can be obtained
at www.ICGtesting.com
Printed in the USA
BVOW08s0944180717
489565BV00003B/8/P